MIRACLES
In The
PITS

MIRACLES
In The
PITS

God Stories from God Speed Ministry Chaplains and those we serve.

RENEE BINGHAM

XULON ELITE

Xulon Press Elite
555 Winderley Pl, Suite 225
Maitland, FL 32751
407.339.4217
www.xulonpress.com

Unless otherwise indicated, Scripture quotations taken from the King James
Version (KJV) – *public domain.*

Scripture quotations taken from The Message (MSG). Copyright © 1993,
1994, 1995, 1996, 2000, 2001, 2002. Used by permission of NavPress
Publishing Group. Used by permission. All rights reserved.

Scripture quotations taken from the Holy Bible, New International Version
(NIV). Copyright © 1973, 1978, 1984, 2011 by Biblica, Inc.™. Used by
permission. All rights reserved.

Paperback ISBN-13: 979-8-86850-717-5
Ebook ISBN-13: 979-8-86850-718-2

DEDICATION

This book is dedicated to the glory of God, the fame of His name. God Speed Ministry was His idea and initiative. The stories in this book are His actions in our lives and in the lives of those to whom we are called to minister. He blesses us by calling us to witness and share in His ministry.

Thank you, Lord God Jehovah!!

ACKNOWLEDGMENT

NONE OF THIS story would have happened if it had not been for the prayers of my husband, Gary Bingham. He prayed us into this ministry and keeps praying us through it. The power of an earnest, heartfelt prayer obliterates mountains and creates momentous opportunities. Thank you.

This book would still be a collection of stories residing on my hard drive if it were not for Chaplain and Author Richard Guy. Rich called mid-2023, just months before God Speed Ministry's 20th Anniversary, asking if we had ever considered publishing a book. He took the initiative to organize the collection of stories into a book and begin creating a story from my random notes. He gave us the motivation and guidance needed to get this done. I am eternally grateful. Thank you, Rich!

To each volunteer who gave their hearts, time, gifts, and resources to the call of God Speed Ministry, thank you. Without the dedicated and faithful volunteers of chaplains, helpers, prayer warriors, and donors, there would be no God Speed Ministry. You are the energy and life of this ministry. You are the hands, feet, arms, voice, and face of God to the racing community. Thank you for overcoming your fears, answering the call, sacrificing time with your family, and enduring long hot days at tracks to share God with the racers you love. You are my heroes.

Thank you to each person who shared their God stories with us the last 20 years. Your stories inspire and encourage us. It is our desire they do the same for everyone who reads them. Thank you for sharing your sacred experiences with others. We originally published your stories in the God Speed

Ministry publications and are thrilled to share them with the world now as a celebration of what God has done through you. Thank you.

TABLE OF CONTENTS

List of Illustrations

Chapter 1

IN THE BEGINNING...

**HOW GOD USED TWO FAITHFUL, OBEDIENT BELIEVERS
TO LAUNCH A MAJOR RACING MINISTRY.**

A Year of Suddenly's

EXCITEMENT FILLED THE air. The brightly colored race cars lined up, each one a masterpiece of design and power. Race cars, adorned with sponsors' logos, gleamed under the bright Texas sun. The teams, dressed in matching crew shirts, worked diligently to prepare the car for its run. The smell of fuel and burning rubber engulfed them.

Drivers had spent countless hours perfecting their skills, fine-tuning their cars. This was their moment, their chance to chase their dreams. The competition was fierce, with seasoned veterans and promising newcomers vying for the top spot.

The event was a blend of celebrations and camaraderie. Fellow racers sharing stories and experiences. Friends and family gathered, their excited voices and laughter filling the air. The IHRA event truly felt like a reunion, a coming together of people who shared a deep love and appreciation for the sport of drag racing.

I looked around at the crowd. Strangers had become friends, bound by a shared exhilaration and a common goal. I recognized this event was not just about winning or losing. It was about the journey, the passion, and the bonds formed along the way.

This camaraderie is the essence of the International Hot Rod Association (IHRA). This was our family. We had once been the newcomer, the outsider. Now 14 years later, Gary was an icon in the sport. Yet he came to prove himself once again in pursuit of a fifth championship. This was his passion, his life's work.

I could not help but feel grateful. Grateful for the thrill of the race and the unwavering support of the racing community. I was grateful that Gary's love and passion for racing had connected us to this family.

While Gary raced, I worked in the control tower as a specialist of the Compulink Timing System. My priority was to enter the information from the tech cards into the driver's class. This information was crucial for the announcers and media to provide accurate and up-to-date details about the drivers and their performance during the races. It was a challenging task, but I took pride in contributing to the smooth operation of the event. It was rewarding to see the drivers receive recognition and their moment in the spotlight.

That Saturday morning March 27, 2004, the San Antonio Raceway control tower was bustling with activity. The Race Director was busy coordinating with the various race departments to ensure the smooth running of the event. The announcers, being the voice of the races, relayed the times and any notable incidents or entertaining moments encountered by the cars during their qualifying runs.

Being in the control tower with such a lively atmosphere allowed me to witness firsthand the excitement and passion of the racers. They would often come to the tower to ask questions or engage in conversations about the event.

Bill Bader and Bill Dickerson engaged in one of those conversations. Bill Bader owned IHRA. He was passionate about life and rebuilding IHRA. His drive for excellence was legendary as proven by Summit Motorsports Park, the Ohio based track he owned. Under his guidance, it became the premier drag racing venue in North America.

Bill Dickerson was a local chaplain with Racers for Christ and ICRA. He substituted as event chaplain for ICRA since they could not attend this event. The International Christian Racers Association was the official ministry of IHRA.

Focused on the task in front of me, I had tuned out the tower chatter. Suddenly, Bill Bader cut through my concentration. "RENEE!" Immediately

I turned to see what he wanted. I knew that tone in Bill's voice from past encounters. Bill had an important, urgent project for me.

Bill Bader looked at me, pointed his long bony finger in my face. "You! You!" He looked heavenward, his face beaming with inspiration. "Perfect idea," he said. "You!" again pointing at me.

"What?" I asked curiously as this was unusual, even for Bill.

"I'll tell you later."

"Come on Bill, you can't do that to me."

"I will tell you later," he said with sternness.

I knew Bill well enough to know the conversation was over. Later was the next day.

Late that night, Gary and I were eating dinner in our motorhome. "Something strange happened in the control tower today," I said.

"Stranger than normal?" He asked and we both laughed because working for Bill Bader was always exciting.

"Oh yeah." I replied and shared the incident.

"What time was that?" he asked as the color drained from his face.

"Around 10:30 a.m.," I replied. "Why?"

Now tears were streaming down his face.

"Gary, what's going on?"

"Renee, I was on my knees in this motorhome, praying for God to show us why we are still racing. I asked for direction, or we would come off the road. We can race around home and help our church. So whatever Bill asks you tomorrow, the answer is YES!"

It was a beautiful, sunny Sunday morning as Bill Bader and I stood on the balcony outside the control tower. Bill shared his thoughts from the previous day.

"Renee, I have thought about the current situation with ICRA. Due to health and financial issues, ICRA is not fulfilling their commitment as

4

I expect or desire. Yesterday I had an inspired idea. You and Gary are dedicated to our mission and have the organizational skills to make this vision a reality. I believe you can create a unique platform that combines our shared passion for racing and our faith in God." Bill said, his voice filled with trust and confidence. "I will give you a year to put it together. I will keep my word to ICRA for this year."

I could feel the excitement building within me as Bill painted a picture of a new ministry. He emphasized the importance of creating a welcoming and inclusive environment, where racers of all levels and backgrounds could come together to share their stories, support each other, and strengthen their faith.

I felt honored and humbled by Bill's trust in me. In my mind, I could already see the impact the ministry would have – racers connecting, being inspired, and finding a deeper purpose in their sport.

I started to say yes as Gary instructed. Bill interrupted. "I want you and your family to pray about this before you give me your answer. You need to consider the impact and the requirements this will have on you and your family. We will meet at the next IHRA national event in April."

As I stood there on the balcony, a mix of emotions flooded over me. On the one hand, I felt a deep sense of gratitude that Bill saw something in me and trusted me with this opportunity. On the other hand, I could not help but feel a bit overwhelmed by the magnitude of the task ahead.

I took Bill's advice to heart and, together with my family, we spent dedicated time in prayer and contemplation. We considered the impact this endeavor would have on our lives and weighed the requirements it would entail. It was not a decision to make lightly, as it would require momentous time, energy, and resources. It would mean sacrificing other aspects of our lives and taking on additional responsibilities.

As the days turned into weeks, I found my heart becoming increasingly excited about accepting Bill's offer. The vision he painted of racers coming together, sharing their stories, and finding spiritual nourishment resonated deeply with me. This ministry had the potential to make a meaningful difference in the lives of those involved.

On Thursday, April 22, 2004, our team arrived at Rockingham Dragway with the intention of starting a new ministry. But that is when we learned God decided to shorten our prep time. I have heard God does "suddenlys" but never experienced one such as this.

We met Skooter Peaco, standing in for Bill Bader. He surprised us by asking how quickly we could put together this new ministry. It turned out that ICRA had not responded to IHRA's attempts to communicate, leaving a gap in providing chapel services for this event. IHRA felt the urgency to make an announcement at the next event in just three weeks' time.

While Bill Bader and IHRA were eager to move forward, they understood the importance of being fully prepared. As Skooter emphasized, "You only have one chance to make a good first impression. Do not blow it." He continued to provide us with more details about the ministry. It would be its own separate entity and the official ministry of IHRA. They promised their support and assistance in promoting our services. They wanted a ministry that they could be proud of, but the timeline was incredibly tight – just three weeks!

The suddenness of the situation was unprecedented, as though God had intervened to challenge us. We would need to work diligently and efficiently to ensure that we were ready to make a positive impact within the given time. It was a daunting task, but we were determined not to let this opportunity slip away.

Gary and I had no experience, no background or education to rely on to create a ministry. Time had been our comfort. To put this together in three weeks, we would have to enlist the help of reliable and supportive individuals who can contribute to various aspects of the ministry. In addition to our daughters Christy and Lisa, Steve and Brenda Corker and Rusty and Theresa Cook became valuable resources due to their experience with racing events and participation in race ministry.

Throughout the process, we had to stay prayerful, seek God's guidance, and be open to His direction. And to remember that even in our limitations, God can work wonders. He would equip us with what we need to fulfill His purpose.

Two days later, still at Rockingham, we struggled to find the right name for the ministry. This first step was critical. Skooter said the name represented the image of the ministry. It should roll off the tongue, be precise, yet tell what we were about.

Our small group brainstormed throughout the weekend between racing and working. The proposed names were: Perfect Light Ministry, Straight and Narrow Ministry, Racers Association of Christians for Everyone (R.A.C.E.). But nothing was definitely 'it.'

At the close of Saturday's race, Aaron Polborn, IHRA Vice President and marketing guru, was leaving the tower. "Hey Aaron, I need your professional opinion." He looked at my collection of names. Nothing was 'it' for him either. As he turned to leave, he said, "If it were mine, I'd call it God Speed."

That was it! Godspeed means 'to achieve one's goal, do well, prosper, to turn out well, to assist and benefit, and to travel rapidly.' That was IT!

Now we could create Bill's vision to please God's heart and serve the racing family by building a community of faith.

As we embarked on our journey to create a new ministry for IHRA, we quickly realized that there was much more to it than we had initially thought. We had focused solely on the chapel services and the need for volunteers, but we soon discovered that there were many other aspects to consider.

First, we had to navigate the world of business. We were naive to the fact that running a ministry also meant running a business. There were financial obligations, legal considerations, and administrative tasks we had not anticipated. We had to learn about budgeting, acquiring resources and managing them effectively.

Additionally, we soon realized that covering all the races in the US and Canada would require a substantial team of chaplains. We had to recruit and train individuals who were enthusiastic about their faith and knowledgeable about the racing world. This required extensive networking and outreach efforts to find individuals who could commit to this unique form of ministry.

Despite the challenges and humbling moments, we remained steadfast in our belief that this was a divine calling. We understood that God often calls us to tasks that stretch us beyond our comfort zones and reveal our limitations. We trusted that He would provide the necessary resources, strength, and wisdom to fulfill His purpose through our ministry. We knew that God had placed this burden on our hearts for a reason, and we were committed to embracing the journey, no matter how challenging it may be.

God met us in that decision. The next week after Rockingham was as miraculous as that moment in the tower. All day Monday ideas popped into my mind. Gary laughed as I shared the ideas that evening. His laugh was one of amusement and wonder. This was bigger than the two of us, but God was preparing the way. We were along for the ride.

All week, ideas rained from heaven. I took 'dictation' as fast as possible. God gave His vision for the ministry, the 'Blessing decal,' an image for the logo, and so much more. It was miraculous.

Roland Osborne authored an article about this miraculous week which he published in his magazine **Christian Motorsports Illustrated**. He titled it, "How to Start a Ministry in 6 Days."

Then...

"Everything is on hold with God Speed Ministry."

That was the email from IHRA, Thursday, April 29, 2004, at 10:00 p.m. ICRA had contacted them. They promised to cover the rest of the 2004 events. IHRA would keep their word to ICRA. But this would be their last year. I would still preach at VMP as they promised but there would be no announcement of a new ministry.

We tried to make sense of the sudden halt after such a miraculous start. We knew that God had a purpose and a plan, but we were uncertain of what it looked like.

We prayed fervently, seeking clarity and confirmation from God. Slowly, but surely, He began to reveal His plans to us. We felt His peace and assurance that this ministry was meant to be birthed, even if it never became the ministry of IHRA.

With this newfound determination, we started to brainstorm and envision what this new ministry could look like. We considered the unique gifts and talents God had given us, as well as the needs we saw in the community.

Our hearts stirred with a passion to reach out to the lost and hurting, to offer them hope and healing through the love of Christ. We wanted to create a ministry that would make a real impact in people's lives and bring glory to God.

So, we took that leap of faith, trusting that God would provide and guide every step of the way. We knew it would not be easy, but we were confident that with God's leading, we could overcome any obstacles. We stepped out in obedience to His calling, knowing that He had something incredible in store for this new chapter of our lives.

Little did we know at that time just how far-reaching and impactful God Speed Ministry would become.

God Speed Ministry was officially established on May 4th, 2004, with the purpose of serving the Lord God Jehovah. In our first year, we provided services at five IHRA events. The first official service was at the IHRA ACDelco Nationals at Virginia Motorsports Park as promised.

During the Mooresville Pro Am, Race Director Satch Gragg asked us to provide a service. People gathered in the grandstands or listened to the PA. At another event we instituted the "Holy Drive-In, where people would drive up in their golf carts or bring lawn chairs to our pit area for chapel service. Journalist Thomas Pope coined the phrase in one of his articles which included ministry at IHRA events. We were asked to provide services at other events, including a last-minute request at the IHRA Fall Nationals at Rockingham Dragway.

At the Mooresville Pro Am, people asked for an offering box, but since the service was a last-minute request, we were unprepared. However, we gave the offering to Satch Gragg, whose son Elliott had leukemia, to help them with medical travel expenses. Fortunately, Elliott was able to beat the cancer.

Supporting racers has been one of the foundations of God Speed Ministry throughout the years. We have provided support to the racing family for various needs, often helping with uncovered expenses during medical crises. One family, for example, had a husband and father battling a rare cancer, preventing him from working. The ministry's support prevented them from losing their house, which impacted their lives significantly.

In November 2004, IHRA announced God Speed Ministry as their official ministry. By the end of that year, we had five chaplains, including Rev. Bill Dickerson and Rev. Jerry Blazier, both of Texas. There was also a children's program within the ministry, led by our daughter Christy.

While we accomplished numerous tasks in terms of the business and legal aspects of the ministry, there was still much to do at the end of the year. Within a short span of three months, we needed to find chaplains for IHRA Divisions One, Two, Three, and Five. We needed essential equipment and resources such as PA systems, uniforms, and offering boxes.

Despite our shortcomings and challenges, the ministry continued to thrive and grow. God provided us with the knowledge and connections we needed at the right time, as well as generous individuals who funded specific needs. God exceeded our expectations and blessed us abundantly throughout our journey.

Looking back, I realized that those few words shouted by Bill Bader had set in motion a journey filled with purpose and impact. Through his passion for excellence and our commitment to the project, we successfully created a ministry that displayed the power of unity, faith, and giving.

God Speed Ministry became a symbol of hope, community, and the remarkable things that can be achieved when we come together for a greater purpose. And I, Renee, am forever grateful for being a part of this incredible journey.

"Renee & Gary Bingham 2005"

Chapter 2

LOOK WHAT GOD HAS DONE

THE BUILDING OF A MINISTRY

In 2005, THE IHRA annual awards banquet took place in Cincinnati, OH. As the new ministry for IHRA, God Speed Ministry began its journey by presenting a Bible to each of the officials at the banquet. This act marked the ministry's official introduction.

As the racing season commenced, Renee made it her mission to ensure the presence of God's Word was felt throughout the racing community. She laid a Bible in every trailer she could access or placed one in the hands of those she encountered.

This endeavor was inspired by the belief that when God's word is shared, it will not return to Him without achieving the purpose for which He sent it, as stated in Isaiah 55:11. God Speed Ministry seeks to make a positive impact and bring the message of faith to the racing community within the IHRA. By sharing the Bible and spreading God's word, we hoped to inspire, uplift, and provide a source of spiritual guidance for those involved in the sport.

This story highlights the impact of God Speed Ministry's mission to distribute Bibles and how it has changed lives. Renee Bingham recalls an encounter at the IHRA Team Finals where a man approached the outreach table and requested two Bibles.

"Ma'am, may I have two of the Bibles you have on that table?" he asked as he pointed to the God Speed Ministry outreach table.

"Sure. Help yourself." I (Renee) said without stopping. I was setting up for chapel service at Piedmont Dragway for the IHRA Team Finals.

Minutes later he spoke again. "Ma'am, may I tell you why I want two Bibles?"

"Certainly." I stopped and gave him my full attention.

"I'm fifty-two years old. I've been in church two times in my life—the day I married my wife and the day I buried my mother. You had a table out at Farmington Dragway. I rode by it and stopped to look. I picked up a Bible and took it home. I began to read it. I met the God of it. He saved me and changed my life.

God Speed Ministry Literature Table

"I gave it to my wife. She read it and met the God of it. He saved her and changed her life. We shared it with our two teenage children. They met the God of it. He changed their lives.

"We've read that Bible until we've worn it out. It's falling apart." He ran his finger across his palm as though tracing a line of scripture. "Ma'am, we've worn the ink off the pages. May I have two Bibles?"

This family's journey with the Bible had left it worn out, with the ink on the pages fading away. The man stood before Renee, requesting two new Bibles to continue their spiritual growth. His testimony serves as a powerful confirmation of the impact of God's Word.

God Speed Ministry has given away thousands of Bibles, and this man's testimony solidifies the importance of their mission. It demonstrates how reading the Bible can lead to a personal encounter with God, transformation, and the salvation of individuals and their families. It serves as a testament to the power and purpose of God's Word in changing lives.

The ministry continued to grow and expand under God's guidance. The addition of Joe and Debbie Sannutti of Georgia, Rev. Floyd and Diana West of Illinois, and Matt Zapp of Ohio helped cover different regions and divisions within the ministry. Deborah Tankersley of Tennessee, joined as a children's chaplain in Division Two, while Rev. Star and his church in Virginia covered Division One. Roger Hallead of Michigan later joined Division Three. Together, these passionate individuals provided services at thirty-four events for IHRA.

God's provision was evident in providing chaplains for every division, including Lisa, the younger daughter, who joined in 2005. Gary and Renee were grateful for the people God brought into their ministry through divine connections.

In March, they asked IHRA for permission to do children's ministry at National Events. "You have your thirty minutes for chapel. That is all." However, through prayer and God's intervention, in October they were able to hold children's services at the IHRA Torco World Finals at Rockingham Dragway. They even added an early service at 7:15 a.m. at the request of racers and vendors who wanted time with God before their day started.

Children's church at IHRA National Events debuted during the 8:30 a.m. service. Christy Rice created the Kids on Track program, which offers thrilling Bible stories to teach children God's values and character. Children enrolled to receive monthly newsletters with Bible stories, puzzles, and games.

Through their ministry at drag races, over twenty new souls became citizens of God's kingdom, with seven saved in one service. Many of these new believers would never have set foot in a church if it were not for the ministry at racetracks.

"Kids On Track Division 5 with Michelle Michael"

To meet the growth, new chaplains answered God's call and more series were added, while still covering all IHRA Pro Am, National, and Jr. Dragster events. Tracks also recognized the need for track chaplains and started programs to build chapels on their premises. Each divisional chaplain worked to build their divisional "church" and reach out to every race team.

The children's ministry received an official name, Kids On Track. Divisions Two, Three, Four, and Nine had dedicated children's chaplains. Children and parents love the lessons and programs alike, and each year, the ministry orders more Children's Bibles and sees an increase in children receiving the Heavenly Herald newsletter. The Birthday club also continues to grow, and the ministry receives heartfelt emails and letters from grateful children.

This is one of our favorite stories from kids.

Broken Tires

"What's this?" two young boys questioned Gary Bingham as he worked on his race car in his pit area. It was Saturday afternoon at the Sooner Nationals in Tulsa, OK. Gary looked up to see them pointing to the Prayer request box on the literature table of the God Speed Ministry display set at the edge of his pit next to the main road.

"That is so people can write prayer requests on the note pad and place them in the box. We add them to our prayer list and pray with you for God to answer them," Gary informed them.

"Oh." They began to talk to each other. Gary went back to work on his race car. He glanced up to see both boys busily writing. Soon, Gary heard the lid of the box clank shut and waved bye as the boys turned to leave.

Later that evening Gary heard excited voices calling to him: "He heard us. He heard us!" The same two boys were rolling used race car tires along the road. "Thanks mister. We got our tires! We got our tires!! God answered our prayers. We got our tires."

"That's great," laughed Gary, smiling as the boys rolled their treasures toward home. Curious about what the boys had written earlier, Gary looked in the box.

"Dear God, we need broken tires."

In 2007, IHRA and God Speed responded to the requests of racers and added a Saturday service at IHRA national events. They experienced miraculous doors opening and many answered prayers. As a result, they now offered four church services at IHRA National events, including a Saturday morning service, two Sunday morning services, and a children's church. The attendance grew. People's lives were changed, and professions of faith were made. Miraculous healings also occurred during the services and through the prayer chain.

IHRA received emails expressing gratitude for the invocations during pre-race ceremonies. Additionally, sportsman racers requested an invocation before their eliminations start, and IHRA approved their request.

God Speed Ministry partnered with Feed the Children. The money collected at IHRA events fed hungry children in the United States. Over the span of 2007 to 2012, the ministry was able to feed over 128,500 American children through the race family's contributions.

Gary and Renee did not originally set out to establish a large ministry but were simply following where God was leading them. They believe that God has bigger plans and ideas than they could have ever dreamed of.

MAKING A DIFFERENCE

"To sum up what God Speed Ministry has meant to me this year... it has been a year of confirmation! I know that as a ministry, we ARE making a difference in the lives of the folks at the events we are blessed to minister at. I have had many racers tell me that they have rededicated their lives. They are now walking the walk, not just talking the talk!! Others have shared that even though they did not raise their hands during the invitation, they accepted Christ as Savior. They are serving Him now! I have seen a seventeen-year-old senior share her faith boldly with her friends, family, and the entire world on Facebook. I have seen racers that two or three years ago didn't acknowledge Christ in their lives, step up and boldly share Christ with fellow racers! As a ministry, we ARE making a difference, and isn't that what it is all about? -IHRA Division Two Chaplain Joe Sannutti

Debbie & Joe Sannutti 2005

"There have been so many beautiful stories of God's love and power touching people," Renee said. "One of my favorites is about a family who was able to attend church together for the first time. The parents had different denominational backgrounds. Our non-denominational service allowed them to worship together for the first time." Renee Bingham

Lisa Bingham Collier and husband Matt created InVISION Youth Ministry for God Speed. It debuted in May 2008. They wanted teens and young adults to know God has something for them too.

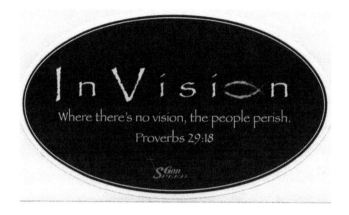

InVision Decal

The name InVision comes from our desire for young people to see God's vision for their lives. We want them to be IN vision with God's will for their lives. We want them to see life, other people, and themselves with God's perspective.

MISSION: To bring youth to a realization of Who God is, the vision He has for their lives, and who they are in Jesus Christ. Proverbs 29:18 states, *"Where there is no vision, the people perish."*[1]

In 2012, the Abundant Life Camp launched. It is an extension of the Kids On Track and InVision programs, only locally. Here, children and youth experience God's Abundant life for a week. Each day each activity intends to demonstrate, inform, and bring the Kingdom of God to bear in the lives of the campers. The three elements of peace, joy, and righteousness, when exemplified, revel the kingdom is present.

---

[1] King James Bible

God Speed Ministry's growth from 2006 to 2010 has had a significant impact on the lives of many individuals. The organization now offers over one hundred services in more than twenty-five states and three major Canadian cities. One particularly encouraging aspect of this growth is the increase in church attendance each year.

Volunteers play a crucial role in the ministry, serving as chaplains, musicians, helpers, and teachers. They generously give their time and energy, often sacrificing vacations with their families to volunteer with God Speed. These devoted individuals travel hundreds of thousands of miles to share God's love with the racing community.

The personal and powerful experiences that people have had with God through God Speed Ministry have been life-transforming. Many individuals have reconnected with God and experienced personal growth because of their involvement with the ministry. One man said, "I thought I came to NC to race but now I know that I traveled all the way from Texas just to hear this sermon today. God used racing to bring me here to hear this message." And another, "You changed my life. I'm back in church and I'm happier than I've ever been in my life."

Through various means of communication, such as newsletters, the ministry's website, and email, God Speed can stay connected with its community in multiple countries. The website serves as a hub for connecting, teaching, sharing news and activities, and sharing prayer needs. Prayer is highly valued within the ministry. Powerful prayer warriors receive prayer requests via email and social media. Miraculous healings have occurred because of the faithful prayers of the ministry's members, with individuals brought back from the edge of death.

At racing events, the ministry prays for hundreds of drivers. Some drivers request prayer before each race. There have been instances where chaplains were asked to lay hands on cars, cast out demons, bless them, and sanctify them. Even skeptics have returned with stories of astonishment and amazement at the power of God. God's presence is truly invigorating and exciting within the racing community and beyond.

Jack Larsen Testimony "This is my testimony of God's love:

"At a local bracket race in Joliet, Illinois I prayed with the track chaplain before round one. (I have never prayed with a chaplain before.)

"During my round three burnout, the brake pedal rod broke, and I had no brakes. If that would have broken off anywhere but where it did, it would have been catastrophic!

"God was watching over me. What a loving God we have!" – Jack Larsen

"God Speed Ministry does so much more than Chapel Service and pray. We desire to add value to every person's life. We know God loves every one of us too much to leave us in the mess we create. He gave His only Son Jesus to give us abundant life. I want to live it, experience it to the max. And I want to share it with you!" – Renee Bingham

This is a reflection on the growth and impact of God Speed Ministry over the course of ten years. The ministry started with only five chaplains and now has sixty-four volunteers who consistently help. These chaplains provide support and encouragement to race teams, officials, and fans in times of difficulty and loss. They are ordinary people who have overcome their fears and doubts to become representatives of God Almighty. Through their work, numerous individuals have come to Christ, with thirty-three salvations in the past year alone.

The growth of the ministry has been possible by the internet, which has allowed God Speed to connect with people across the nation and world. It also facilitates better communication with chaplains and enables a worldwide prayer chain, which is the backbone of the ministry.

The ministry is thankful for the support of the International Hot Rod Association (IHRA) and the individual support of IHRA and track staff. These staff members go beyond to accommodate the ministry's services, sometimes sacrificing their own comfort or sleep to do so. The ministry is grateful for their support and wants them to know how much we appreciate them.

In 2014, God Speed Ministry became the official ministry of the new Professional Drag Racing Association and Loose Rocker Promotions, solidifying its status in the drag racing community.

SURPRISED BY GOD

God surprises me in so many ways. Some are amazingly simple. There was the morning I was driving to an early meeting. I made a wrong turn as I concentrated on my speech for the meeting. It was miles later before I realized what I had done. Now I will arrive later than desired. I was berating myself as I neared a stop light. As I sat at the stop light I looked into my rear-view mirror. There was the most spectacular sunrise coming up over King's Mountain.

"That's for you," I heard God whisper. "You have never seen it from this angle before and I wanted to share it with you. I direct your steps."

I often need reminders like that. God gave me a grand one as I was preparing the "State of the Ministry" address for the GSM Conference in January. I began compiling numbers for events, locations, and attendance. I felt urged to create a visual. Let us see how far God has broadened our reach over ten years.

I started with a basic map of the US and Canada. I colored all the states and provinces where IHRA has a sanctioned track. Then God directed me to do the same thing with a world map to see all five countries where IHRA sanctions tracks. He urged me to add the states and countries where we are mentoring people online and by mail. I WAS STUNNED! Until that moment I had no idea how far God was reaching through this ministry. See for yourself in the photos. Look what God has done!

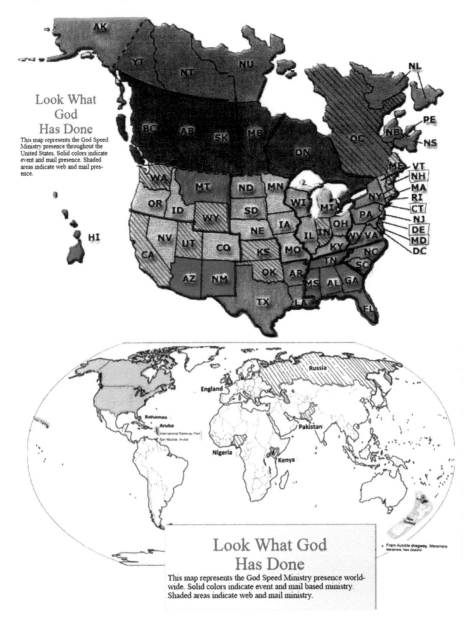

Look What God Has Done

This map represents the God Speed Ministry presence throughout the United States. Solid colors indicate event and mail presence. Shaded areas indicate web and mail presence.

Look What God Has Done

This map represents the God Speed Ministry presence worldwide. Solid colors indicate event and mail based ministry. Shaded areas indicate web and mail ministry.

These numbers and the stories from those we serve demonstrate God's power through our obedience. In October 2012, three chaplains heard amazing God stories. The lives of these individuals were completely transformed by their encounter with Christ Jesus. They met Jesus at a drag race or other event where God Speed Ministry held chapel services.

One.

W was one of the biggest baddest Hells Angels around. When he was just twelve years old his dad took him to a bar where his dad was to fight another man. He left W outside and put a sawed-off shotgun in his hand.

"I am going in there. If I don't come out alive, you kill the man when he comes out. Don't let me down." W's dad came out alive, but W's life progressed heavily into that violent lifestyle. He became undefeated in fights. He became known as the biggest baddest hells angel around.

Other hells angels came to fight him to prove their reputations among the clubs. He remained king and had the scars and appearance to show. Once the police stopped W. W beat all four officers single-handedly. No one was standing when W finished.

But at an event early in 2012, W met someone more powerful than the "church of the hells angels" and stronger than W himself. W met Jesus Christ. He wept openly and professed Christ as Lord, repenting from a life of crime, violence, and intimidation. All the power and energy W expended in the service of the devil is now harnessed and transformed into service of the kingdom of God. He now one "big bad dude" for God!

Two.

The young man swung his scooter around, circling back to Renee. "I have a story you need to hear. My uncle used to race with me but had to stop when my aunt became ill. While taking care of his wife, he bought and sold equipment. The police confiscated one of the pieces of equipment he sold to another man. My uncle, a good Christian man, did not know the equipment was stolen merchandise. He took out a loan to repay the man he sold it to.

"Then he went back to the man who sold it to him. The man promised to pay him back. He never did. Anger and bitterness grew. One day he told his wife, 'When you die, I'm going to find that man and kill him.'

Months after my aunt passed away, I was able to convince my uncle to return to the races with me. We went to chapel service at Rockingham. God used your sermon with the apple and fork illustration, to change my uncle's intent to kill the man who wronged him. Two lives were saved that day. Best of all, my uncle was restored to Christ."

Three.

Larry Langley is a TS racer from South Florida that I (Joe Sannutti) led to the Lord earlier this year. He told me that not too long after, he was praying. He said "Lord, if this Christianity is for real, would you please give me a sign?" He said that he walked out to his mailbox a little later and there was a package from God Speed Ministry! He said that was all the sign he needed!

***

Since the singular focus of IHRA in the beginning, the ministry has grown. We now cover seven racing series: The IHRA (International Hot Rod Association), The PDRA (Professional Drag Racing Association), the WDRA–World Drag Racing Alliance, Loose Rocker Promotions, the SWJDA (Southwest Junior Dragster Association, the CCRA (Carolina Class Racers Association), Staging Light Events, and the Hornet's Nest Auto Fair. This diversification of racing series demonstrates the ministry's ability to adapt to different forms of racing and cater to a wider range of racers and fans.

Overall, the 2020 recap for God Speed Ministry displays the ministry's growth and success in broadening its reach within the racing community. With its expanded coverage and partnerships, God Speed Ministry has solidified its position as a spiritual authority in the world of drag racing.

The 2020 pandemic disrupted the status quo for the face-to-face ministry. We only held twenty-eight in person services. GSM leadership saw it as an opportunity to minister in a new way.

We turned to digital ministry to continue to minister to our community of faith. On Easter Sunday 2020, God Speed hosted the Epic Easter Event. Each GSM Chaplain had fifteen minutes to share a message during the three-hour event. We broadcast on Zoom and Facebook Live. Thirty people joined in the Zoom room and 3,999 on Facebook Live. Our first ever live internet event was a massive success.

Social media platforms increased our outreach significantly. In 2020, we reached 264,143 people online and in person. In 2021, we recorded 502,252 touches with people around the world in eleven countries. In the years 2005 to 2019, our total reach was 43,371. Now we have reached over half a million people in one year!

This growth in reach and impact happened by our strong online presence. We have established active social media accounts on platforms such as Facebook, Instagram, Twitter, and YouTube. We consistently post devotionals, inspirational quotes, updates on racing events, and messages from our chaplains to engage with our audience.

Additionally, we have upgraded our digital ministry through the launch of the new GSM website. This platform serves as a hub for our community, providing resources such as online sermons, articles, and prayer requests. It also allows individuals to connect with our chaplains and join various racing communities.

Impact of last 17 years

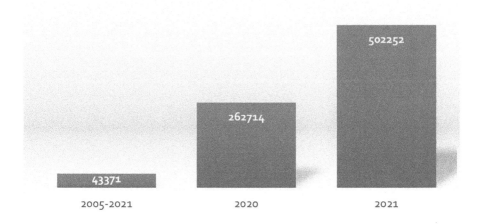

	502252
262714	
43371	
2005-2021	2020	2021

Looking ahead, we aim to further enhance our digital ministry and continue expanding our reach. We are exploring new avenues such as podcasting and live streaming racing events to engage with our audience in innovative ways. As we move forward, our mission remains the same – to share the love of Christ and provide spiritual guidance to those involved in the racing industry.

"I'm grateful to God and each person who supported God Speed Ministry these past twenty years," said Renee Bingham. "The journey and growth of this ministry far exceeded my expectations. The prophet Isaiah said, 'There will be no end to the increase of His government[2],'" Renee started. Gary added, "God is the God of growth and multiplication. Hold on. The best is yet to come."

---

[2] Isaiah 9:7 King James Bible

The mission of the ministry, based on Isaiah 61:1-3, is the organization's heartbeat. Renee believes what God has done so far is just a drop in the bucket. "This ministry is a testament to God's faithfulness," Renee added. "I can't wait to see what God will do next!"

Chaplain's Log

God Speed Chaplains share God-driven experiences.

God Connections: A Prisoner's Last Request
Renee Bingham & Joe Sannutti

At one of our Ministry Conferences around 2010, Renee told us a neat "God Story" about awesome "God Connections".

At the time, Roland Osborne was the editor of a quarterly magazine "Christian Motorsports Illustrated." In 2005, he had published an article on God Speed Ministry with an in-depth look at how God used Gary & Renee Bingham to create God Speed Ministry in six days.

Part of Roland's outreach ministry was to give copies of the magazine to prisons across the U.S. One of these magazines fell into the hands of a prisoner who was serving a life sentence for murdering a young lady. This prisoner read the article and when he did, he got an idea. This prisoner sent a letter to God Speed Ministry asking for help.

His son's thirteenth birthday was approaching. His son loved NASCAR racing but had never been to a race. Could God Speed get tickets for his son to attend the Daytona 500? Remember, we engage in drag racing, not NASCAR, so there is no connection there.

Then this prisoner gave his reason for asking.

His relationship with his son was broken. His son wanted nothing to do with him. His dad was a murderer in prison. His mother, a strong believer in God, had died of cancer recently, even though the church had believed and prayed for her healing. Someone in the church had even told this young man, "If your faith is strong enough, God will heal your mom." When his mom died, he believed it was his fault. What a burden to place on a twelve-year-old!

He was mad at himself, the church, and God. The boy was now living with his grandmother who was praying for help.

The son's relationship with God was broken. This prisoner's last goal in life, before being executed, was to see his son restored to God as he had been. He believed if he could make a way for his son to go to the Daytona 500 from prison, it would demonstrate to his son how God still answers prayers, even when we have committed horrible sin. He wanted his son to know God loves, forgives, and restores.

Renee had no connections to anyone in NASCAR. She called the basic number of Motor Racing Outreach (MRO) based in Charlotte, NC, just fifty miles from God Speed Ministry. They told her their ministry is to the drivers and teams but gave her Roger Marsh's name and phone number. Roger is the president of National Fellowship of Raceway Ministries (NFRM) whose outreach and ministry is to the fans, event campers and day attendees.

Renee called Roger, telling the story and the reason for the request. Roger said this was certainly something they would be glad to do. Renee thanked Roger and his staff. She hung up and thanked God for making a way for this boy to enjoy his thirteenth birthday and prayed for his restoration to God.

Her part was finished. It would be years later before she would hear the "rest of the story" when Roland shared it at the conference mentioned at the beginning of this story.

As Renee was finishing the story, we were all amazed at how God had made all these connections, from Roland's article to the prisoner, to Renee, to MRO, to Roger Marsh with National Fellowship of Raceway Ministries and his staff.

All to give a thirteen-year-old boy, who no longer had his dad in the picture, the experience of a lifetime.

All the attendees were all reflecting on this neat God-Story about God Connections. We marveled how much the Lord is concerned about our wants, not just our needs. Then Roland stood up and said, "Renee, aren't you going to tell them the rest of the story?" Renee did not know there was more to the story.

The Rest of the Story by Roland Osborne

ROGER MARSH PASSED the request from Renee to his team at Daytona. They contacted the grandmother and made the arrangements. Someone would pick them up and take them to the Daytona 500.

God exceeded the prisoner's request extravagantly. The boy not only attended the event but was taken into the infield and introduced to the drivers and teams by the lady who was their escort that day. She escorted them around the different areas of the track. In other words, she made it a wonderful, unforgettable experience for the young man and his grandmother.

But God was not finished.

As the lady drove them home, the grandmother shared about the boy's father making these arrangements from prison for his son's thirteenth birthday.

"Why is he in prison?"

"He murdered a girl."

"My daughter was murdered."

God began to reveal the connection between this boy and the lady whom God ordained to be his escort to the NASCAR race. The lady in Daytona that put this entire package together for this boy and his grandmother, this same woman that escorted them all around the racetrack and made sure that they were comfortable and had a wonderful time...was the mother of the young lady this boy's father had murdered!

As a believer, she had forgiven the man who killed her daughter. She had also prayed for God to give her an opportunity to share her forgiveness with the man's family.

Suddenly...a God-Story about God connections became an awesome God-Story about forgiveness!!

Jim Edlin God Connection

By Chaplain Joe Sannutti

Joe Sannutti

On Saturday of the 2014 Immokalee IHRA Pro Am Race, during the first round, we had a rain shower.

I backed my truck up to the God Speed tent and strapped the tent to the bumper, so it would not blow away. As my wife Deb and I sat in the truck with the A/C running, I looked in the rearview mirror and saw two men sitting under the tent. Concerned that the diesel fumes might be bothering them, I got out and went back to ask and I noticed that one of them was in a wheelchair.

I introduced myself and asked if the fumes were bothering them, to which they replied, "Not at all." We struck up a conversation and I found out that the man in the wheelchair is long-time drag racer named Jim Edlin, from Michigan. Jim used to race Mopar's in the IHRA Stock Eliminator Class and had bracket raced up until just the last year.

Last March, Jim was diagnosed with pancreatic cancer, and went through surgery that did not get it all, then chemo and radiation...still did not get it all. His health kept going downhill and he was placed in hospice care recently.

Jim's last wish was to be able to see one more drag race before he passed on to heaven (Jim is a Christian). The only race in the US was the IHRA season opener down in South Florida. So, with that in mind, Immokalee it was. His son, Jim, along with a friend of his, Rob, pulled the back seat out of Jim's van and bolted down Jim's easy chair, so that he could travel with his feet elevated. They then proceeded to "break him out" of hospice. They drove non-stop nineteen and one half hours to get to Immokalee. When they left Michigan, it was cold with snow on the ground. They detoured around Atlanta, traveling through Birmingham and Montgomery, trying to avoid the mess in Atlanta from the "Great storm of '14".

When they got to Immokalee, Jim sat in his wheelchair by the fence and watched every pair of cars go down the track. His good friend Pat O'Connor, who has lived one mile away from him for forty years, flew out from his winter home in Phoenix, Arizona to spend the weekend with him. His sister who lives on the East coast of Florida also came to the track to see him.

Backing up just a bit... as we sat under the tent talking during the rain shower, Pat had mentioned how he felt that this was a "God Connection." We talked about how God sent the rain shower and how they "just happened" to come up under our tent and how the Lord orchestrates these connections. I shared one of my favorite testimonies of "God connections" and we just had a fun time of sharing.

After visiting with them for thirty or forty minutes through the rain shower, I felt like I had known them my whole life. When the racing resumed, I got an idea and wondered if it would be possible for Jim to make a trip down the drag strip. I went to the tower and shared the story with our Race

Director. I asked if it would be possible. Frank Kohutek said absolutely. They would make room for us to do it between rounds.

Frank then generously gave me the keys to his car, which just so happens to be a Mopar...Jim's favorite vehicle! I went downstairs and asked Pat if he thought Jim might like to make a pass with me. He said, "Oh yeah! I bet he will. Let me ask." When Pat leaned down to ask him, Jim's face lit up like a child on Christmas morning! I got one of those big ol' lumps in my throat.

I brought the car around. His son, Jim Jr. helped him into the car and got him strapped in. We went to wait our turn to make our run. As I pre-staged the car I looked over at him and he was still grinning! After the run when we got the Elapsed Time (ET) slip. I looked at it and saw we had run a 10.35 ET, but by the look in Jim's eyes, you would have thought it was a 4.90 pass! After I handed it to him, he tried to hand it back to me. I told him it was his to keep. Once again, that smile was big and bright!

When we got back to the pit area, his son was waiting with tears in his eyes from seeing his dad with that huge smile on his face. To tell the truth, my eyes were sweating a little, also.

As they got Jim out of the car, I could not stop thanking the Lord for allowing me to be there to experience such an awesome time. Jim stayed up near the fence until well past dark and then it was time for them to leave. As they got ready to leave, we gathered, joined hands, and had prayer.

I never got to see my new friend here on this Earth again, as he passed away just over four months later, but I KNOW that I will see him in Eternity! Godspeed, my friend!

One more "God Connection" that I will never forget!

PDRA: Faith, Family and Racing

By Lisa Collier

There is often a reason for celebration at the racetrack. Each event, winners are crowned, and someone goes home with a shiny new trophy and some hard-earned cash. It is one of the main reasons we show up at the track week after week. But most are quick to also realize that though cars and speed are part of the passion, it is the people who make it all worthwhile. And even when we celebrate a performance, it is really the people behind the accomplishments we are cheering on.

One of the Professional Drag Racers Association (PDRA) mottos was fully lived out at the recent Firecracker Nationals, as people celebrated in a whole new way. PDRA owners Tommy and Judy Franklin have never been shy about their faith in Jesus Christ, often incorporating it into their various activities. A church service is offered at every PDRA event through God Speed Ministry and each event opened with prayer.

At the beginning of this year, chaplain Tommy D'Aprile suggested holding baptisms at an event. People quickly began responding and a date was set.

Eight people were baptized at the Firecracker Nationals, held at Virginia Motorsports Park on Saturday, June 30. It was the first time such a celebration was held at a PDRA event, and one that will not be forgotten any time soon by all in attendance.

"I saw God moving, and I believe we should do it more often at the races," D'Aprile said of the baptisms.

"People feel comfortable around their racing family. So cool."

"The PDRA is all about faith, family, and racing," stated Judy Franklin. "So, when Tommy D'Aprile and Renee Bingham came to me to ask if we could do water baptisms at our Virginia race, I said absolutely that is a great idea! The opportunity of doing water baptisms at a PDRA event–let alone at our racetrack–was something that we dreamed of! I feel that God has put Tommy [Franklin], the girls, and I in the drag racing community for this reason, to bring others to Christ!" The baptisms really hit home for Tommy and Judy Franklin since their youngest daughter was one of the eight. "We were blessed to watch our youngest, Ashley get baptized at the race! Let me tell you, tears were rolling, and we were so happy to watch her make this decision! Tommy D'Aprile is such a wonderful mentor to our Junior Dragster drivers, and we had at least six of our junior drivers get baptized that day."

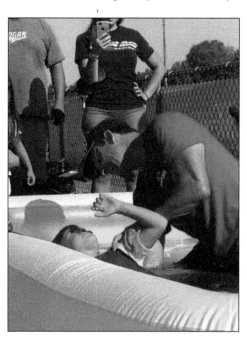

People took to social media to share their thoughts on what happened that day:

"I am most thankful for God Speed Ministry, Renee Bingham, and Tommy D'Aprile. I am watching my kids accept the Lord in a whole new light. They go to Church with me on Saturday mornings because they enjoy it, yes ENJOY it. It is fun, it is upbeat, it is real life. PDRA puts God first and is faith driven. This organization has done so much more than turn on win lights for my kids, it has brought them closer to God; it is making them BETTER PEOPLE and for that I will forever be grateful!"

"The PDRA is impacting the lives of people. I am one of them, but there are many. To have a professional racing organization that puts GOD first with a FAMILY based atmosphere. I am very blessed to be a small part of the PDRA, but I am HUGE benefactor of what GOD is doing through this organization."

"I have been trying to tell people this for three years now. The PDRA is absolutely the best racing organization anywhere. From our first race three years ago at Rockingham Dragway when Renee Bingham started praying on the starting line for the Ronnie Davis crash. I think every person on the property was on the starting line praying with her. Now we look forward to Saturday mornings with Tommy D'Aprile. God has truly blessed us with our racing family."

"There were ninety-eight people at church at 8:15 a.m.," added God Speed Ministry President, Renee Bingham. "Several people had testimonies of what this meant to them and the differences their baptisms made. We love being a part of the PDRA and amazing celebrations like this."

"What a great testimony to what the PDRA family is about- loving and supporting each other in all that we do," added Judy. "We are looking forward to doing this again at a future event. We have the pool in our motorhome for anyone wanting to get baptized. You can do so by reaching out to Tommy D'Aprile or Renee Bingham!

"We all love this sport of drag racing, but it really is about something bigger than drag racing!" (July 24, 2018)

Man Down!

By Renee Bingham

"Man down!" was the call.

It happened so quickly, so unexpectedly. We, Chaplains Keith Petersen & Renee Bingham, responded immediately. I knew there was no wreck, so what was wrong?

As we arrived, we saw a man flat on the track and heard the emergency crew calling life flight. I rushed to his side. It was Marc Kinton, IHRA Safety Director. He had critical head and shoulder injuries suffered when he crashed his four-wheeler. He was air lifted to the University Hospital.

Chaplain Keith took Marc's uncle Robert Kinton, also an IHRA Official working the event, to the hospital. Keith stayed until Marc was stable. He returned with Robert around 1 a.m. on Sunday morning. Keith was preaching at 8:15 a.m.

After the service Keith headed back to the hospital to check on Marc. Before he left the track, word came that Marc was being released! What?!! How?!!! Only yesterday he was presumed dead when we found him on the track. We were thankful he was alive but knew he had a long road to recovery. Now, praise be to God, he was being released from the hospital.

Keith took him clothes and shoes, picked him up and helped him into the hotel room. He then went to get his pain prescription filled.

"Man down!" was the call. It happened so quickly, so unexpectedly, less than twenty-four hours from the first. Again I, Renee, responded since Keith was still with Marc. This time it was Thomas Czaplicki, another IHRA official. He had crashed his scooter on the return road while responding to a wreck on the track. He too had head injuries and a hurt shoulder. Since he was conscious and talking, he was transported by ambulance to the very hospital just vacated by Marc.

"Keith, I need you to return to the hospital. Stay with Thomas. He is alone."

Two hours later we at the track were still waiting for word on Thomas. When Keith called the news was dire. Thomas was extremely critical. Life and death decisions had to be made quickly. They were asking Keith to make them since he was the only one there with Thomas. He wisely called IHRA.

Skooter Peaco, IHRA Vice President, quickly began making calls to family to inform them of the accident and seek choices on treatment options. I talked with Thomas' wife, trying to calm her while answering questions.

Scott Gardner, IHRA President and aid Dan Driscoll went to the hospital immediately. Keith stayed with them until late Sunday night. When he returned to the track near midnight, he went to staging lanes for the remainder of the race. That is the heart of a servant.

Keith visited Thomas on Monday. Dan stayed in Canada with Thomas until he was released on Friday. They flew to Virginia, Thomas' home, where he was admitted to the hospital.

Both Marc and Thomas are alive and recovering. They, the emergency crew and IHRA have all voiced their appreciation to God Speed for the presence of chaplains during that critical time. The presence of a chaplain reminds them that God is there and gives consolation and hope. That is why we serve.

STANDING IN THE STORM

by Tommy D'Aprile

THE MEDIA HAD us all dead to rights before Hurricane Irma even came to the Florida coast. I kept in constant contact with my prayer partners and prepared as best I could for the storm.

Weeks before, Renee and I had been talking about the power of prayer. Many Christians do not realize the power they have through the blood of Jesus. We tend to pray weak prayers and beg instead of proclaiming by the blood. Many Christian brothers and sisters do not realize they have this power.

Well, here it was the day of the storm, and the media had been hyping this up as the media usually does. I chose to stay and stand firm on God's promises. I proclaimed that the hurricane would not harm us and that it would break up as it neared our county. With hands lifted and the promises of God I continued to thank Him for the deliverance He would show me this day. I quoted Exodus 14:13 *"Stand firm and you will see the deliverance the Lord will bring you today."*[3]

I knew the power in testimony this would have and was excited to share this victory before it even came. The storm raged on and as the eye of the hurricane approached, I grew stronger in faith, casting out fear and keeping the devil under my feet. By His mighty power I could feel God working. I prayed and thanked God for the storm to die and thanked Him for my family's safety. I was bold enough to ask to keep our power as well. I continued to look at the radar images on my phone. The storm headed right for us. Then suddenly the storm started to get disorganized. The once perfect

---

[3] New International Version (NIV) Holy Bible, New International Version®, NIV® Copyright © 1973, 1978, 1984, 2011 by Biblica, Inc.®

eye broken apart. I have pictures of these radar images as well. The storm weakened and I could hear the weatherman say, "We don't understand it, but the storm is losing organization." As the media does though, they said it would strengthen again. The storm now had lost its eye and the heavy areas of wind and damaging flooding had moved to the east of us, right before it was to hit my county.

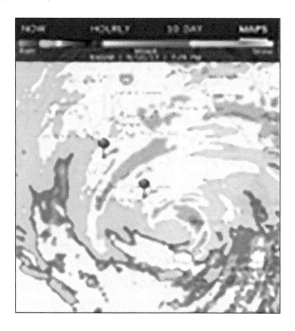

Weather radar of Hurricane Irma

The power flickered here and there and when it did, I got bold again and proclaimed victory. Through it all I lost some of the screens on my pool cage, all of which needed to be replaced anyway. A tree in my back yard, which was too tall for me to trim, was trimmed for me with the branches laid on the ground beneath it. We kept power while much of the county was without. My kids and sister, in different parts of the county, all kept power as well with no damage to houses or property.

This storm was life changing and faith building. I know the power God has given us and I know we can defeat the devil and his schemes. The question is, do you? Faith, not fear, will bring God's deliverance. *"As for me and my house we will serve the Lord."* Joshua 24:15[4]

One of the biggest things I had to do was keep negativity away. Anyone who spoke defeat, especially the media, was turned off. I focused on God and said NO to the devil's schemes. Not just during hurricane season, but every day we must stand firm, know the promises, and power we have by the blood.

---

[4] King James Bible

THE SKIPPING CD

By Chaplain Joe Sannutti

ONCE WHEN I was in Tucson, Arizon, after a long day at the track, I went to the Waffle House near my motel for a late supper. I was still wearing my God Speed Ministry shirt. My waitress asked about the ministry. While we were waiting for the meal to cook, we chatted about the ministry, the Lord, and life in general. As I was finishing my meal, the waitress came back to my booth and asked if I had time for a God Story. Of course, I said sure.

She then asked if I believe that God could cause a CD player to skip. That was an odd question, but I said "Ma'am, I believe that God can do anything He wants to do."

She then began sharing about her grandson who was four years old at the time. She said that every day she goes to her daughter's house on her way to work. They usually chat for a while, drink a glass of tea or a cup of coffee, and then she goes to work.

One day she said that they were in the kitchen, drinking coffee when the CD player in the other room started skipping on a song. She said that they waited a little bit, thinking that it would stop skipping and go back to playing the music.

When it did not stop, she got up to fix it. When she got to that room, she thought she heard a muffled sound coming from her grandson's room. She opened the door to see her grandson hanging from the post of his bunk bed with his feet about six inches off the floor. She ran to him, picked him up, and got him to start breathing again. He had a towel around his neck like Superman's cape. When he jumped or climbed off the top bunk, the cape got caught and his feet slipped out from under him. He was choking to death.

When she finished, she was crying, I was all choked up. When I finally cleared my throat, I said "Yes ma'am, without a doubt... God CAN cause a CD player to skip."

Keeping it Real with Joe Sannutti

By Lisa Collier

God Speed Ministry's Division Two covers most of the southeastern US. It thrives within the heartbeat of the Bible belt. Chaplain Joe Sannutti and wife Debbie have led Division Two for eleven years as head Chaplain and Children's Chaplain. Together they have built relationships, led dozens to faith in Christ and encouraged countless people through trials. People close to Joe and Debbie remark on how well these two practice what they preach, opening their lives to people and reaching deep into their hearts. Recently Joe had major health issues but has bounced back incredibly well. He says he is "blaming it on the Lord" and "feels like a million bucks" and wants to thank everyone for the prayers.

"One of my favorite things about serving Division Two is how close knit we are, even though it's a big Division," Joe said. "My prayer is to see people in Division Two be discipled, to really get involved in their walk with the Lord daily. Of course, my prayer is always to see more folks come to Christ." It is easy to see that the folks in Division Two have a real love and concern for each other, from chaplains and racers to track owners and organization staff. Division Two is home to several God Speed Chaplains including Children's Chaplain, Deborah Tankersley, Memphis International Raceway Track Chaplain, Kenny Bomar, and PDRA Chaplain Tommy D'Aprile.

Back when I was the track chaplain at Montgomery, Alabama, the track operator found out that he would be losing the lease. He told us that the next race would be his last race. At the track chapel service that weekend we had about seventy-five people and I told them what I had been told, and it got emotional. We did not know if anyone else would pick up the lease.

We heard they were going to turn the track into a Target distribution center. So, we thought this would be the last time we were all gathered in the same place. We had really formed a neat bond over the years. It took twenty minutes for people to leave."

"This one guy named Paul hung around until everybody had left. He walked up to me, and he said, 'I just need to tell you something. When you first started preaching here, I never came to the chapel service for the first year, but I watched you. I watched you race. I have seen you when you win. I have seen you when you lose. I saw you when you were helping a competitor. I have just watched you. What I have seen is, you are real.'"

"I was already emotional and that just really got to me. I told him he would never know how far he reached down into my heart, because that is exactly what I try to be–real. Folks, we must realize that everywhere we go people are watching us, and sometimes they are making 'eternal decisions' based on what they're seeing."

Joe Sannutti has not always embraced the 'chaplain' title. Like most of us, his path to Jesus had a few obstacles turned steppingstones. One thing is for sure, everyone in Division Two is sure glad his road led to that of race chaplain.

"I started racing back in the mid-seventies. My favorite car back then was the '68 Nova. It was tough on the strip. Now, though, it must be one of them fast dragsters. I love the Top Dragster Class," Joe emphasized with a smile. "The eye-opening thing about being in ministry is that folks are watching us when we don't know they are," he went on to say. "One of the sweet parts about it is that so many of the folks know us from racing prior, and that opens the door for us sometimes. They know us. We are not coming in with a suit and tie and squeaky-clean fingernails. I have just been blown away at how the Lord has impacted folks through this ministry."

"At the IHRA Team Finals last year at Carolina Dragway, South Carolina, I had a guy come up to me and ask if I preached the message at Darlington Dragway, South Carolina, about five years prior. He even remembered the topic of the message. I told him that was me and he said, 'Well I was there. At the end you asked if anyone wanted to give their heart to the Lord or rededicate their lives. I did not raise my hand, but let me tell you, the following Wednesday night I was in church. Sunday I was in church. As it is right now, I am teaching a class on Wednesday nights, and I am teaching the boys. I got myself back involved in church.'"

We may not know it, but people who hear a message at the racetrack are changed."

Joe came on board with God Speed Ministry in January 2006, covering the southeast and races as far as Arizona. Over the years, Joe and Debbie have seen God at work repeatedly, although it has not always been an easy road. They have had to balance family, businesses, health concerns and make a myriad of sacrifices to serve Division Two. They have gladly laid themselves aside to take on this role.

"One of my favorite God stories would have to be the time when nine out of twelve folks that came to the Tucson Chapel Service accepted the Lord," Joe vividly remembered. "That was the time that I slept under a table in the airport on the way out there. The plane had problems. They would not rent me a car. They said there was something wrong with my license. I had just flown across the U.S. with that license, but they said it did not look right to them. The IHRA safety meeting, where I was to pray over the event and the staff, was supposed to be at 11:00 a.m. and I got to the track at a minute till eleven, running on about four hours of sleep since four o'clock the morning before. We had chapel service the next morning. We did not have but twelve folks show up, but nine of them made a profession of faith. It was like the Lord was saying, 'You may have to sleep under a table, miss a couple of planes and fight a battle, but just be obedient.' I am not saying this with false humility: It was not me. It was not even a salvation message. It was more of a message of encouragement."

"Folks were just hungry. It was phenomenal. "Here is what it takes to be effective in six words: Love God, love people, be real. Honestly, that is it. That's it in a nutshell."

The "Bill"ding Blocks of a Kingdom Legacy

Chaplain Bill Dickerson

They say everything is bigger in Texas. That is true for drag racing as much as anything. Texas racers race hard and win and lose big. They also join as family, like drag racers often do. But in Texas there seems to be a different kind of bond, one not easily broken and one that stands the test of time and trial. Among this area's racers there are a large number of people who love Jesus. You will know this because they are sure to tell you. They are unashamed, bold, and love God's truth.

Although God Speed Ministry's home base is in North Carolina, God Speed really began in Texas. It was at the National Event in San Antonio where Gary and Renee Bingham first received the call to begin a ministry. Soon God Speed Ministry was formed as the Official Ministry of the IHRA and the task of covering every race in each division loomed large – a true God-sized undertaking.

Thankfully, we serve the One who is faithful, and He had great plans. Even before God Speed Ministry was a thought, race ministry was alive and well in Texas, thanks to the diligent work of Chaplain Mike Fulfer. Through him the Lord was grooming just the person to lead Division Four as their race chaplain.

Mike was the Division Four Racers for Christ (RFC) Chaplain and had already begun the legacy of pulling others alongside him to serve in ministry. One of those individuals was Bill Dickerson. In Bill's own words he explained, "Twenty-three or so years ago Mike Fulfer had convinced me to be a chaplain at Houston Raceway Park. I had my first service there at a national event. I continued there until Glen and Dee Brabham opened Lone Star Raceway in Sealy, Texas. I started racing there in the late nineteen-nineties.

"Later an IHRA western division was started. I began as a chaplain and then became Divisional Chaplain." Bill was serving in Division Four when he met Gary and Renee Bingham at an IHRA National Event in San Antonio.

"Bill Dickerson was present in the tower when Bill Bader felt the urge to ask Gary and I to create a ministry for IHRA. He called me the very first week of God Speed Ministry's existence. He interviewed me rather than me interviewing him!" Renee remembers with a smile on her face. "Bill would have nothing to do with this ministry unless it met God's criteria as described in His Word. I passed his test. Bill became the first divisional chaplain for God Speed Ministry."

One of his greatest strengths is the ability to pull others alongside and equip them for further ministry. Such was the case with Division Four Kids on Track for Jesus Chaplain, Sylvia Maedgen. Sylvia combined her love of kids, skills from children's ministry in her home church and her passion for supporting her husband Tommy's racing habit when Bill approached her about offering kids church at the Division Four events.

"Tommy and I met Preacher Bill in Odessa, Texas at our first IHRA race back in March 2000," Sylvia shared. "Preacher Bill asked us if we were racers and he and the guys started talking about racing. Before we left, he invited us to church service the next morning. We attended with less than a dozen people that Sunday morning. It was cold and windy. We have not missed a service since that time."

Since then, the Lord has moved in Division Four. Sylvia has often had more than a dozen at kids' church alone. "The priority is to tell the children about Jesus by using the scriptures. The focus is Jesus, and that is important. Some the kids do not attend church at home. It is important that they hear about Jesus somewhere, and this is an opportunity for me and God Speed Ministry to provide that service to them. It is so true that God blesses you double, triple, and more when you follow and serve him. My life has been blessed more than I had ever dreamed possible.

"We have an exceptional group of people in Division Four. Preacher Bill has done wonderful things in growing the participation of racers to attend church services. We have had racers get sick, or pass away, or family members get sick, and we all come together to help each other out and support each other. Preacher Bill makes those connections with racers and keeps everyone informed of what is going on with each other. God is doing splendid work in Division Four. Preacher Bill and God Speed Ministry are true disciples."

Bill has also cultivated track chaplains throughout Texas. Jerry Blazier serves at Lonestar Raceway, Steve Longmire at Abilene Dragstrip, and Jim Wilburn at Dallas Raceway Park.

When Jerry became a Christian, the Lord asked him to leave his former life behind, and that included racing. Later, the Lord gave him permission to join his two greatest passions in life- Jesus and cars. He has served with God Speed Ministry since 2005.

Western Conference Chaplains

"Giving some small portion to others for what Christ has done for me is my greatest blessing," relayed Jerry. "Anything I can do for Him is a small return of gratitude for what He has done for me on the cross." When Bill was unable to attend the IHRA event at San Antonio in 2013 Jerry and the other chaplains pulled together to cover the event. Thanks to the depth of chaplains in Division Four there was no issue in making sure the event was fully covered.

"Bill has taught me that you don't let age, you don't let aches and pains stop you from doing what God's call you do to," Jerry added. "He serves with a passion. He loves the people he serves. But most of all he loves that he has a position of trust in their life that he can bring the truth to them, even if it is not pleasant. And they still love him for it."

"Over the years racers have come to know that God Speed Ministry and Bill Dickerson are going to show up and the attendance at the services has grown," Jim Wilburn reflected on the impact of Division Four ministry. "Bill is sincere and has love for everyone. At the last IHRA Pro Am race, toward the end of the service, racers were shouting 'Praise God,' and it was a good time."

Steve Longmire was inspired to start a ministry at his home track after hearing Bill preach the IHRA Divisional Team Finals in 2003. "I met Bill at the Division Four Team Finals in Shreveport, Louisiana in 2003. I went back and talked to him after the team finals in 2004, and he got me on the path to becoming a chaplain. I chose to serve with God Speed because I love cars and racing, and I love the Lord. Put all of that with the fact that I spend time racing with my family and friends, and you have the Triple Crown. It is rewarding to do what you love with who you love and serve the One who is Love.

"Serving as a God Speed chaplain lets me share the good news with others in a comfortable setting, outside of the traditional church. It has let me bring God out from the four walls people think can hold Him in and introduce him to some old drag racers."

Steve continued, reflecting on the impact Bill has had on him personally and in Division Four: "Bill has always encouraged me to be real, and not pose as something I am not; this is not as easy as it seems when the powers of darkness come at me. Knowing that I have Bill in my corner is always comforting, because when I slip up or fall, he reminds me to keep the faith and respond in a Christian way the way Jesus would."

When Tulsa Raceway Park in Oklahoma was added to Division Four, God orchestrated the meeting between Bill and a young man passionate about racing and Jesus. "I met Joey Keith and encouraged him to be a track chaplain," Bill added. "Now this is how things come full circle. This last weekend, May 2-4, Joey served as RFC chaplain at Dallas [Ennis] for the NHRA Division Four event, and according to Tommy and Sylvia did an outstanding job. It is God's circle. We just get to ride in it."

Besides serving with both RFC and God Speed Ministry, Joey also has his own ministry, Christian Outreach Racers Evangelism, or C.O.R.E.

As the legacy of Division Four race ministry continues to grow, transform and bring people to the knowledge of their loving Savior, we say a big Texas-sized thank you to Mike Fulfer for laying a foundation and to Preacher Bill and his supportive wife Jean, offering hearts of gratitude to the Lord for their tireless service, truth, friendship and love.

Steve Longmire concluded, "His legacy is God's legacy; all who seek the Good News are welcome, and loved in the grandstands that are directly under heaven. No walls, no dress code, no judgment, just hope, faith and glory. A big happy family worshiping together, racing together, and growing together, because of the faithful vision of men like Bill Dickerson."

The Ultimate Air Ride

By Renee Bingham

"Ladies and gentlemen, this is your pilot speaking. The weather service advises us that there is very turbulent air in the forecast for today's flight. For your safety, we ask that all passengers remain buckled in their seats for the first hour and the duration of the flight. No one is to be out of their seats for any reason. If you need to go to the restroom, go now before we pull away from the terminal. We apologize, but we cannot control Mother Nature. We will do our best to make the flight as safe and bearable as possible. Beverage service is suspended for this flight as well. Thank you."

I do not fly much, but I knew this was not a normal procedure. I wondered just how bad it would get and pondered the possibility of danger for the aircraft and passengers. But even as these thoughts began to enter my mind, another thought replaced it: "Cast your cares upon me, for I care for you."

I had been reading and studying about the blood covenant of the Old Testament as well as the Blood of Jesus and all it means for the saints of God. I had just finished reading the testimonies of hundreds of people who had pled the Blood of Jesus over their families and possessions during some of the worst natural disasters in U.S. history. They, their homes, businesses, and personal effects were supernaturally saved when everything around them was heavily damaged or destroyed.

I bowed my head. "Father, I thank You that You love me. Thank You for Your word that tells me of Your protection. Thank You for the blood covenant that protects Your children. Father, I plead the blood of Jesus over this airplane and all its passengers. Send Your angels before us to prepare the way."

The final preparations were made, and the aircraft began to taxi onto the runway. Everyone took a deep breath. Everyone was tense, waiting for the expected turbulence. I was grateful that this was the largest plane I had been on in any of my flights.

The plane gathered speed and began to lift off the runway. The takeoff seemed normal enough to me. We continued our climb, still no turbulence. We reached our cruising altitude, and everything continued normally. Everyone relaxed slightly and began to turn their focus to their books, music, and other interests.

Thirty minutes into the flight, the Holy Spirit began to direct my attention back to the ride of the flight. Most flights have the usual motion of movement as well as the general vibrations of air travel, but there was none of that, only smoothness, a silkiness in this flight. It was like sitting in a chair in your living room, no movement.

About that time the pilot came on the speaker again. "Ladies and gentlemen, we are turning off the seat belt sign. You are free to move about the cabin. Fortunately, the weather forecasters were wrong. Beverage service will begin shortly. Enjoy your flight."

I smiled to myself. God had answered my prayers. I just love it when God gets to be God in our lives. He so wants to be here for us, but He also waits for an invitation from us. If we want to solve our problems ourselves, He will allow it. But He has already laid up everything we need for this life. It is available to those who believe and ask according to His will and way.

> *"And they overcame him by the blood of the Lamb, and by the word of their testimony; and they loved not their lives unto the death."* Revelation 12:11[5]

---

[5] King James Bible

Again, the Holy Spirit brought that scripture to my mind and emphasized the "word of their testimony." I knew that God had done His part, now it was time for my part. A covenant involves two parties and has conditions for both parties.

I looked at the gentlemen on either side of me. One was looking out the window and the other was asleep. "Later," I thought. At that moment, there was a ripple of movement by the plane. God was reminding me of what He had protected us from and that I had a part in that scripture as well.

"It's really beautiful out there, isn't it?" I commented to the gentleman looking out the window.

"Yes, it is," he replied.

"I am glad we can enjoy the view because the ride is so smooth. In fact, I do not think I have ever been on a smoother ride in all my life."

"Yes, it is smooth," he agreed, but then added as a rationalization, "The weathermen deal with so many variables that they can't always be sure."

"True, they do deal with many variables. But I am glad that God is always sure."

He looked at me quizzically, and then agreed with a smile, "Whatever happened, this is the ultimate air ride!"

MIRACLE T-SHIRTS

By Renee Bingham

AT THE REQUEST of our people, God Speed Ministry has new t-shirts. They have the logo on front and the large decal logo with "*I pray for good fortune in everything you do, and for your good health—that your everyday affairs prosper, as well as your soul.*" 3 John 1:2[6] on the back.

Part of the delay in getting the T-shirts was funding first things first. I had delayed as long as possible. If we were going to have t-shirts this year, (and there was demand for them and ministry opportunities through them,) it was now or never.

When I was pricing the shirts through Doug Herbert Performance Center, who does some of the T-shirts for the National Hot Rod Association (NHRA) pro drivers. The price was unbeatable. Doug Herbert donated the first order of shirts. Larry McLaughlin paid the screening charges. The order was ready in only three days! Thank you, Doug! Thank you, Larry!

At the IHRA Kinston Pro Am in Kinston, NC, Brian Thompson and crew wore their new God Speed t-shirts all the way to the winner's circle. I am not saying the shirts had anything to do with the results, just that it was great to see the shirts get so much exposure their first race out.

By the end of the IHRA Mountain Park Pro Am in Kentucky, we were already out of two sizes and low on a couple of more. It was time to reorder, just weeks after the initial order.

Again, I called Doug Herbert Performance Center. This time I really needed to know the price before I ordered the quantity. Getting the regular

---

[6] *THE MESSAGE: The Bible in Contemporary Language*
Copyright © 2002 by Eugene H. Peterson. All rights reserved.
THE MESSAGE Numbered Edition copyright © 2005

price, I placed the order. When the call came back to confirm the order and delivery date, the price was substantially lower. Thanks again, Doug!

When the shirts came, I pulled out the check book to pay for them. When Larry McLaughlin handed me the bill, he said, "Don't worry about it, it's paid."

"What?" I questioned, stunned.

"The bill's paid."

"How? Who?"

"He did it," Larry said smiling and looking heavenward.

I did not understand.

Larry began to enlighten me. "When I heard that you had ordered more shirts, I told Bob Bratton to give me the bill and I would pay it. Then I prayed, "God you know I am doing this for them to bless them. You also know that things are kinda tight right now financially. Could you help me out with this?"

"That was the 2nd of July. On the 4th of July, I built a transmission for a guy. I made enough to pay half the bill for the T-shirts. The next day, a friend called me with a way to make more money. That covered another fourth of the bill. The next day, Michelle (Larry's wife) called me at work to say the item I had for sale on eBay had sold. That covered the rest of the bill with $5 left over."

"So, He paid for it. I was just the delivery guy," Larry grinned.

I stood there amazed at Larry's faith and what God had done. God is so faithful to His word. Faith pleases God and when we step out in faith, God is then able to work in our lives. What an impressive God we serve! What an impressive testimony of faith!

What miracle t-shirts!

A Day of Miracles

By Renee Bingham

It is a day I will remember forever. It was a day of miracles, not one or two, but six miracles witnessed by the multitudes.

God Speed Ministry was hosting chapel service that Saturday morning of the PDRA Spring Nationals at Rockingham Dragway. We were in the 'upper room' on the third floor of the control tower.

Miracle #1 Provision

In the opening prayer requests I told of the need for a member of the race community who needed life-saving surgery. He had to have $5,000 to pay the surgeon in four days. He still needed $3,500 of that $5,000. A member of the congregation gave the entire amount! Other people gave toward other expenses. In one split second the need was met and exceeded.

Miracle #2 Power of Prayer

We then mentioned Wesley Jones who had fractured the L4 vertebrae on Friday in an accident. As I finished praying for him, I opened my eyes. I blinked several times as I was looking at a man who looked like Wesley. But I thought he was in the hospital with a fractured back. We were on the third floor. "Look at that! You pray for the man, and he walks in the door," said Bob Harris of the PDRA. People were in tears at this point.

"I don't know what God is up to today, but you better buckle your seat belts and hold on for the ride of your life," I said to the congregation as I turned the service over to Chaplain Tommy D'Aprile who was to bring the message.

MIRACLE #3 PROPHETIC WORD FROM THE LORD

Tommy preached a sermon on the "Power of our words." Later we realized it was prophetic. He gave us warning about using our words to tear people down rather than building them up. He urged us to use that power for good rather than evil. We would all see that lived out in the afternoon.

MIRACLE #4 LIFE BREATHED BACK INTO RONNIE.

During the final qualifying round, Top Sportsman racer Ronnie Davis, a perennial winner, multi-time world champion and seasoned veteran driver, crashed his car in a horrific wreck at the quarter mile of the dragstrip. The car became air-borne and went over the guard wall. I responded immediately. It seemed an eternity before Bob Harris and I got there.

Ronnie was unconscious, no pulse, no breath. The safety crew were already working to revive him. I reached my hand into the car touching his. I commanded life to Ronnie while praying to God to help him. Then I moved out of the rescue team's way.

There were small groups of people around the accident scene gathered in prayer. A few minutes later I was able to reach inside the car. I was careful to stay out of the way of the EMT's and safety crew as they continue to work on Ronnie. I laid my hand on his head. I prayed and commanded life once more.

The safety people were top-notch and working frantically. Once Ronnie was removed from the car, they were able to do more intense CPR. They moved him to the ambulance.

People were crying. Some were praying. Chaplain Tommy D'Aprile and Racers For Christ Chaplain Scott Trent were praying with people, comforting them, and speaking hope.

Then word about Ronnie came from the ambulance: "We have a good blood pressure." I turned to tell everyone. He was alive and had good blood pressure.

"That's my God! That's my God!" I cried.

As we were praising God the second word came from the ambulance: "He's breathing on his own!"

MIRACLE #5 IAN STILL HAD BOTH LEGS.

While praying for Ronnie while he was still in the car, I learned about an individual who was hit by Ronnie's car. I ran to him. I knelt by his head as the EMT's worked on his lower body. I laid my hand alongside his face and introduced myself. His blue eyes rolled up and a smile lit his face.

"Hey Renee."

"Ian?!!!"

"Yeah, it's me."

Ian Tocher was a motorsports journalist who was taking finish line photos of the race cars. He was alongside the concrete guard wall of the race track when he was hit by Ronnie's out of control car. It was indeed a freak accident.

I prayed for him. Ian was air lifted to Chapel Hill UNC Hospital. I prayed for him on the ground, in the ambulance, and on the way to the chopper. He was always alert and conscious albeit critically injured. Only later would I hear of the extent of his injuries. But at the scene I heard they expected him to lose both legs before the end of the day. We prayed for complete restoration.

Ian still had both legs at the end of the day. (Months later, Ian had part of one leg amputated due to complications.)

MIRACLE #6 WORDS OF HOPE AND PURPOSE OVERCAME THE EVIL WORDS OF DEATH.

There was a somber atmosphere over Rockingham Dragway as Bob Harris and I returned to the tower. PDRA canceled the day's activities. Racing would resume on Sunday. Everyone in the tower and in the pits were concerned about our two friends. They had major, major injuries to overcome.

Sometime after 3 p.m. different people in the tower, me included, started getting text messages and instant messages saying Ronnie was dead. The rumors continued to build until someone posted "Official message" stating Ronnie had died. Everyone in the tower knew better but seemed powerless to stop the viral lies on social media.

Then my phone rang. It was RFC Chaplain Scott Trent who had gone to the hospital with Pete, Ronnie's friend, and crew. He and Pete had just been in to see a very live Ronnie who was fighting for his life. Scott had prayed for him and felt the power of God descend like never before in his life.

I asked Bob Harris if I could make an announcement over the PA system.

"Yeah, go ahead," he said despondently.

"Attention in the pits, attention in the pits. I want everyone on this property to stop what you are doing and listen to me. Stop what you are doing and listen to me. Ronnie Davis is alive! He is alive! I am on the phone with Chaplain Scott Trent who is at the hospital with Ronnie. He is alive. I need each one of you to get on your cell phones, on social media and put an end to the lies circulating that he is dead. I do not bury the living, and neither should you. Do you hear me? Ronnie Davis is alive. He is fighting for his life. We should be putting our words into prayer for him and positive thoughts rather than burying him when he is trying to live! I want each one of you to join me in front of the tower, in the staging lanes to pray for Ronnie and for Ian. They need our prayers and support."

A river of humanity started toward the staging lanes. I continued to talk over the PA system as people poured into the lanes and in front of the tower. Then I asked them to join hands and pray with me. I asked them to repeat the words of the prayer after me as we prayed for Ronnie and Ian.

Praying for Ronnie and Ian

God came down in might and power as we prayed. All felt the power of unity which created an atmosphere God chose to inhabit. That event stands out above all others in all my years of walking with God and doing ministry.

Words of hope and purpose overcame the evil words of death. Words of unity invited God into our midst personally and powerfully.

Yes, Saturday April 16, 2016, was a day of six miracles at Rockingham Dragway. God answered the prayers of those who believed Him to be the ultimate authority and asked Him to have the final authority. God did exceedingly abundantly more than we dared dream. That is my God!

Author's Note: Ronnie Davis was taken to Moore County Regional Hospital in Pinehurst, NC after his wreck at the 2016 PDRA Spring Nationals at Rockingham Dragway. He was later transferred to UNC Medical Center in Chapel Hill, NC. Ronnie died on Sunday from injuries sustained in Saturday's crash. Godspeed Ronnie.

America Is the Hottest Mission Field

Renee Bingham Tuesday, August 15, 2006

My heart is at the breaking point. Gary and I had the opportunity to minister at the Junior Dragster Nationals in Maryland International Raceway this past weekend. Since it was a national event for Juniors, we did the Kid's On Track Treasure Hunt program for the children. Little did I realize what would transpire as the weekend unfolded.

God gave Christy Rice, God Speed Children's Chaplain, the idea for the treasure hunt to introduce God to all kids (spectator and race crew) at IHRA national events. These hunts are like a scavenger hunt, complete with a treasure map and a varying number of clues. This weekend Christy had prepared clues for the Ten Commandments.

I went race trailer to trailer inviting people to church, handing them a bulletin, and telling them about the treasure hunt. The children were excited to pick up their maps and first clue at the God Speed display. At the display, we also put out Bibles free to all who will take them. The Bibles were designed for pre-teens, teens, and young adults. The Bridge New Testament has a wonderful color graphic of the way to salvation.

We had twenty-nine at church service at 8:15 a.m. Sunday morning, which was good for an event of this type. Three children came to collect their treasure packs. One young man gave his heart and life to God.

But then....... As I stood in my clown makeup and costume (Transforming Love was the title of the sermon) cleaning up after the service, two small girls began calling to me, smiling and giggling. I went over to their pit area in response to them. They were thrilled that "Happy the Clown" had come to see them. We talked and had pictures taken.

Their grandmother came to tell me that they had their treasure hunt clues but were still working on the bonus clues. I went to get their treasure packs and brought them to them. Their grandmother told me they had all been trying to fill in the bonus clues at the bottom. "They" turned out to be this grandmother, her two grown children, their spouses, and all their children. Three generations collectively could not fill in the blank to complete the ten commandments. They had even sought help from others.

With extreme clarity I realized just how far from God this nation we love has departed from God.

And then.... Gary was at the motorhome waiting for other children to come collect their treasure packs. Another grandmother brought her grandson to pick up his pack. She told Gary they had picked up 'books' on the display table. They had been reading them and really liked what they were reading. She wanted to pay him for them.

He told her they were free and hoped that they would continue to enjoy them. She donated to the ministry so we could continue providing these "books" for others. She did not even know that they were Bibles.

Our hearts are so burdened for people. Gary and I cried on the way home once the shock of the morning wore away. We both grew up in church from infancy. We have known no other life. Had God not moved us out of the "church" and into the race community, we might have gone on being so blind to the needs and hurts of the people so lost without God. They have no knowledge of him. We knew and cared about the lost. But now we KNOW! It is personal!

I know about foreign missions. I grew up on stories of foreign missionaries. I thrilled to their adventures and the power of God. But I am here to tell you that America is the hottest mission field, and it is right outside our church doors. Gary said it best, "Don't take this wrong but the evangelist and traveling singers don't need to be going into the churches. People outside the walls of the church need to hear. Our churches are missing the greatest opportunity in the history of God's kingdom. Lost people are mostly not in the churches."

We were missing that opportunity too. Thank God, He moved us. We must go. We have to reach as many as we can."

Pray for churches' eyes and hearts to open.

Pray that churches find ministry outlets outside the four walls of the church.

Pray that we are simply conduits of God's pure love–no pre-conceived ideas of our own.

Pray for more workers in God Speed and every avenue.

Pray for the lost.

Jesus said, *"The harvest is plentiful, but the workers are few. Ask the Lord of the harvest, therefore, to send out workers into his harvest field."* Luke 10:2[7]

---

[7] New International Version (NIV)
Holy Bible, New International Version®, NIV® Copyright © 1973, 1978, 1984, 2011 by Biblica, Inc.® Used by permission. All rights reserved worldwide.

THE WRECK

By Gary & Renee Bingham

MY HUSBAND GARY and I were returning from the IHRA national event in Bradenton Florida. We were traveling up I-75 north of Sarasota. It was dark, very dark. We noticed people pulled over on the side of the Interstate. People were getting out of cars and a semi-truck. Gary moved over to the left lane to give them space. I turned my attention back to the road in front of us. There just one hundred feet in front of us, was a car sideways in the middle of the Interstate. It was flat black. There was no chrome, nothing to reflect light. I screamed and Gary immediately jerked the car back to the right but there was no way we could avoid hitting that car.

I was praying, "Lord, have mercy! Lord, have mercy!"

I saw the lady's face sitting in the passenger seat of the car. Her look was one of sheer terror. She was watching as we were about to hit them.

"Lord, have mercy!" I screamed again.

Somehow, we missed that car! I do not know how. It seemed impossible.

Now my prayer was, "Lord, have mercy on the people who were behind us," and "thank you Lord, that we were safe." I continue to pray for those on the road behind us, then to thank God for our safety.

At this point Gary looked in the rearview mirror and he could see the lights of cars as they were spinning wildly. He said, "it is not good. It is not good," repeatedly as he saw the cars wrecking behind us.

It all happened so quickly, and we were in shock. We realized we had travelled too far to stop. We were over a mile away. We knew we could not get back to help. I called two of our chaplains to begin to pray for the people in the sideway car and for the cars whose lights Gary saw in his rear-view mirror. We knew it was a major wreck.

I began to pray in great earnestness. I had a vision of Jesus walking among the wrecked cars. I saw him touch a lady's leg that was bleeding and saw it healed. I saw him walking from car to car touching and healing the various people.

We were so full of adrenaline we could not sleep, so we drove all the way to the Georgia state line before stopping in the wee hours of the morning to get a hotel.

The next morning, we began to check traffic reports to find information about the wreck. We found numerous reports but nothing about what we had experienced and witnessed. For the next few weeks, we kept searching for information about the wreck. We never found anything.

During that time, as Gary and I were talking about the incident, he said, "You know we did not miss that car. We hit that car Renee, but we did not hit it. We went THROUGH IT. I saw the lady's face in the car as we were about to hit them. Their terror was real. But Renee, we DIDN'T hit them. We went through them like you see on those miracle shows."

God saved us that night. He answered prayers for us and for others. I look forward to hearing the rest of this story when we get to heaven.

Broken Shoulder Miracle

By Renee Bingham

I WAS HURT. IT was bad. But I also knew my only medical treatment would be a sling.

I was lying in a heap on the ground in Ocala, Florida after the rug on the step of the motorhome slipped. It propelled me six feet out and four feet down to the asphalt on my left shoulder. I could not move. I called Gary, my husband, for help.

"I'm hurt. It's bad," I said repeating the words I had heard by Holy Spirit. "My only treatment will be a sling," continuing to say what I had heard. "There will be no surgery, no pins, no plates."

Thus began the journey to a miracle.

X-rays revealed I had snapped the ball of my left shoulder from the shaft and impaled it down over the bone of my upper arm. It was dislocated and skewed which shattered the backside of the shoulder ball.

The hospital sent me to an orthopedic surgeon who told me surgery was my only option. "Without surgery," he said, "you may get a little movement in your lower arm. But you will never raise it. And travel is out of the question. You will stay in Florida for two weeks after the surgery."

After hours of prayer, and Gary reminding me of what I had told him, "My only treatment will be a sling," we began the journey home to North Carolina. It took us three days. We traveled until I could tolerate the pain no more. I could only take Tylenol due to allergies to pain medicines.

We saw Dr. Johnson, a sports orthopedic surgeon, on Monday. He too said I should have surgery and thought the prospect of no surgery would leave the arm useless. He ordered a CAT scan for Wednesday and a return visit for Thursday.

At home I would lie on the sofa with healing scriptures and music playing for hours while wearing a magnet above the break. My natural health doctor suggested the magnet to draw blood to the injury. It was all I could do since movement was excruciating. But it was the best thing I could do. I still knew there would be no surgery and I would have full use of my arm again.

On Thursday Dr. Johnson said, "I have bad news. You are not a candidate for surgery. The interior of the ball of your arm was voided by the impaling. There is nothing to put pins or screws into. Your only option is a shoulder replacement. We may as well let it heal and see what you get."

I was rejoicing. He just confirmed what Holy Spirit said to me while on the ground in Ocala, Florida the week before.

At the seven week appointment the x-rays revealed the miraculous work of God. Left is the photo at the emergency room. Notice how far the ball is out of the socket. Right is the arm today. It moved back up into place through the pull of the magnet and the bones have knit together. Now after therapy I can raise my arm over my head. I am well on my way to 100%. This is a documented miracle!

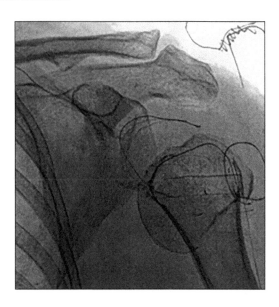

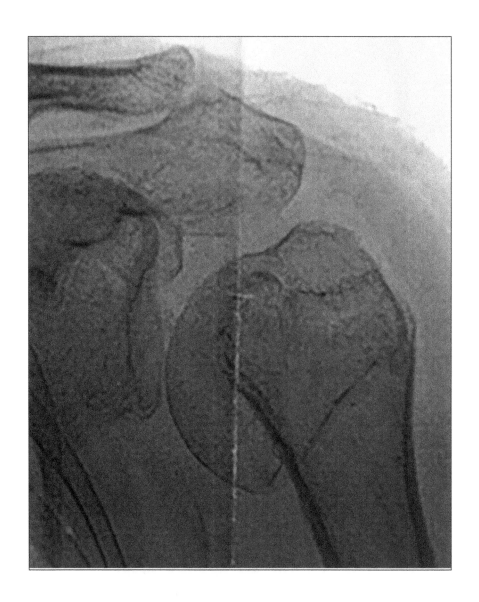

Chapter 3

GOD STORIES

GOD STORIES BY GOD SPEED MINISTRY CHAPLAINS

CHIC LaNASA

Chic LaNasa and Mike Imhoff

MY NAME IS Chic. I love people. I love to share my stories with people.

I remember years ago, I had a friend named Darrell, a young guy, in his twenties. I always shared the things I loved with the people I spoke to.

He was an interesting young man. He loved the Lord. He was a brand-new Christian. I just shared the things God put on my heart to share with him, things in scripture, things about life in general. He was a needy young man. I shared the love of Christ with him.

The strange thing about life is that you hang with people with similar interests. This young man was brand new in his life with a Christ. I just shared the love of Christ with him. He had a desire to do something in life and was searching how to serve Christ in ministry.

He moved to Texas. Years later, I got a package from him. In the package was a picture he had hand drawn and painted of a scene. There were trees on a beautiful hillside. It touched me very much. He had signed it in the corner.

I had only shared with him a few times when he was here in Ohio. He was now a pastor serving in a church in Texas. He had a family with three children. He thanked me for all the things I had installed in his life, which I do not even remember half the things I told him.

But in life, we share with people and do not even realize the impact we have on their lives, that the Lord has on their lives through us. It is just an honor to be serving the Lord. He uses us in ways that we sometimes do not even realize. Later, our rewards will come. Sometimes they do come into this life, others in the next life. I encourage you to always share the love of Christ, every chance you get. Do not worry about putting everything in order. Share every time you get the chance. The Lord will reward that.

Darrell went on to serve the lord. So let that tree of life, and the fruit of the Spirit spread throughout the world through you that He may be glorified. – Chic LaNasa

Gene Head's God Story

WE WERE STAYING at a hotel several years ago. It was Sunday morning. I had on my "These are my church clothes" T-shirt. One of the girls there at the hotel saw it and started laughing before I got to her. She stopped me and asked me about it. I explained to her about God Speed and what we do at the racetracks.

She acted like she thought I was lying. She said, "I didn't think they had church at the races."

I thought it was interesting that something as simple as a T-shirt could give you the opportunity to talk to people about God and share things with them, they have no clue about. I thought it was kinda neat.

Note: Gene and Pattie Head faithfully ministered with God Speed Ministry for many years. Gene was in the 'helps ministry.' He helped set up church service. He helped Pattie with Children's ministry. He helped clean the display and pack it away at the end of the events. He helped wherever he saw a need.

Not all chaplains preach with words. Some do so with acts of service as Gene did.

GLENN HEAD

Glenn Head

I USED TO RACE with Rick. He was a good Christian guy. He was all into faith. He was the guy who mentored me just by the way he lived. He lived the same as he talked. He passed away a few years ago from cancer.

I attribute part of my faith and how I live to his example.

Years later, his son called me. He said, "I have some things of dad's I thought you might be interested in buying. He has the same type of car as you." I told him to bring it by and I would look at it.

So, he comes by, and we are looking at it. He brought it up in his dad's truck. As we are looking at it, he starts to tell me, "This was dad's truck that he drove while he was sick." He said, "when I jumped in, your CD was in the player."

I was in a Christian rock band. He was not a rocker, but the fact that he had influenced my life so heavily, and now to find out that he was listening to my music, and I had an influence on him, really touched me.

It just amazes me to know that is how God works.

I have seen that so many times for some of the youth I work with. We do not know if the person next to us is looking at it as inspiration or help. Just to live the life God wants us to live it and be that example is amazing.

So, to have someone like Rick, who influenced me so much, be influenced by me, was amazing.

LISA COLLIER

I WANT TO SHARE a little bit about the kid's ministry we have at God Speed. When we started this a little over ten years ago, we had kids who were little: two to five years old. When you are pouring into these kids at that age, it is hard to see the impact that you can have on someone so young. It is hard to see the fruit when they are that little.

But now here we are ten years later, on the other side of it.

We have kids that are in college, who are grown up. They are living out their faith. Not only can we see the fruit of what is happening in their life personally, but these kids are going out into the world. We can see the impact they are having on other kids at the racetrack, in their homes, their colleges, even in their own families.

Some of these kids are the only real Christians in their families. It is amazing to hear the stories of the strength that they possess. To think we have had a small part in instilling the love and truth of Christ in them, is a blessing to us. I have found them to be such a blessing. I see how much they are willing to live their lives for Christ, even when nobody else around them is.

I want to encourage you, if you have little ones at home, or if you are in the ministry with young kids, and you cannot see the fruit day-to-day, God is still working. When you plant the seeds, He is going to honor that.

FRAGMENT
By Lisa Collier

Matt & Lisa Collier

A fragment. Incomplete. Unfinished.

Missing a piece, lacking, diminished.

A sentence without a subject, without a verb.

Standing alone, seemingly of little worth.

An engine, but no wheels.

A theme park without the thrills.

A vision, but no plan.

A proud, but solitary man.

A fragment each one.

None complete on its own.

Yet together each one of us is a piece.

And placed within another's reach.

When we pool our resources, our minds, our love.

We complete the picture drawn above.

A glance at this section of life

And all we see is unnecessary strife.

Yet we can trust in a greater plan.

That will not be carried out by a single man.

A part may seem small and insignificant.

But God has a plan for even the ant.

Each one of us is a piece in life's great puzzle.

Each one needed to ease another's struggle.

Maybe when we look, we see only a piece,

But each one is needed to make the picture complete.

MIKE IMHOFF

Chaplain Mike Imhoff

I WAS DOING CHAPEL at a track where we minister. After the service, a guy came up right after the service was over. Everyone knew him but me. Chic (LaNasa) comes up and says, "you need to pray for him."

I started praying for him and was just overwhelmed with how much God loved him. And I just could not get over it. I stopped praying. I said, "you know God loves you so much. He has a plan for your life. It is going to be amazing all God wants to do with you."

He left. People came up and asked if I knew who that was. I said no. They begin to tell me he was one of the biggest...well..." he is really into pornography big time."

I said "oh!"

It impacted me for the next six months of how much God loved him, no matter the sin he was in. That did not stop God's love, or the plans and purposes God had for him.

A couple of years later I ran into him at another track. The first thing he said to me was, "I am so blessed."

I was just taken aback by it. "Wow! That does not sound like the man I heard about."

He took off, and I did not see him again.

I called Renee (Bingham). She said he had come to the Lord in that period. He was now doing online Bible studies. His whole life was turned around.

God loves everybody. He said he loved the world. He gave his only son Jesus to reach out with his love to see him change lives.

"You Saved My Life"

By Mike Imhoff

WE WERE AT US 131 Motorsports Park in Martin, MI at the IHRA Northern Nationals. A young man, late twenties, stopped me in the staging lanes and said, "You saved my life."

I said, "I don't know what you're talking about, but I did not save your life."

"You prayed for me, and I am healed!" He continued. "I had a rare blood disease. Ninety percent of the people who have it die within 2 years, and of those who survive only 2% make it past 5 years. You prayed for me, and I am healed."

I said, "It was not me who saved your life. It was Jesus."

We had been covering events at that track for 15 years, sometimes three events a year. I prayed with a number of people. I do not even remember praying for him, but it is not about me.

OUR MIRACLE WORKING GOD
By Mike Imhoff

MY BROTHER HAD an engine built by a local engine guy. In the process, he mentioned that his wife had cancer. The local doctor sent her to the James Cancer Center at Ohio State University. There they diagnosed it as stage four breast cancer that had metastasized. They sent her home saying there was nothing they could do.

Norwalk Raceway Park (now Summit Motorsport Park) used to run bracket races on Wednesday nights. We would often attend. Her husband did as well. On the last Wednesday of the year, I asked the husband if I could pray for his wife. (I had been praying for her in my prayer time.)

She was sitting in the pickup truck. I shared the story of the man at US 131 Motorsports Park and told her God was still a miracle working God. I prayed with her. Then we both went on our way.

About three months later, my brother called me all excited. He had talked to his engine guy. The guy's wife had gone to the doctor, and she was cancer free!!!

That was three years ago, and her blood tests still show no cancer.

Glory to God. Jesus is still a miracle working God. We just need to be brave enough to act like it.

THE CAMERON MIRACLE

By Chaplain Bill Dickerson

IT WAS THE week before the 2006 IHRA National Event in Tulsa, Oklahoma. Scooter & Jaime Choate were preparing for the event until their five-year-old daughter Cameron got a spider bite. They took her to the doctor on Monday. He prescribed antibiotics and sent them home. She did not get better but worse. By Saturday, she was in the hospital in Waco, Texas. Soon, she was transferred to Cook Children's Hospital in Fort Worth, Texas.

All her friends in the Division Four racing community were praying for her. Word came that she had Leukemia. We all knew she was a fighter. Now we knew why she was not able to fight the spider bite infection.

Saturday's activities at Tulsa were canceled due to the weather. My wife and I left the track to go visit her at Cook Children's Hospital. We found her family gathered around an extremely sick little girl. Cameron lay in a coma on a ventilator. I prayed with the family for Cameron.

We left for home on Monday and started a prayer chain. Tuesday afternoon I got a call from Alan Savage saying the doctors could do no more. Cameron's only hope was God's intervention. I prayed, then informed the prayer chain. Late Wednesday afternoon May 30, another call came. Miraculously Cameron's organs and blood showed improvement. God was at work!

On July 13th she came home to a parade. This was the first time she had been home since the battle began in April. Cameron is a warrior, as are many of the kids fighting so-called adult diseases.

Meanwhile, back at the Division Four Lufkin Raceway points meet, a donation jar had been set up to help the Choate family with Cameron's medical expenses. By mid-afternoon Sunday, there was over $3700 in that jar. In the final rounds of the race, a challenge was issued to all racers and attendees by Tony Gray. "Here is $600. Beat this in donations to the family."

Texans do things big, and they do not back down from a challenge. They rose to the occasion.

There were already T-shirts on sale. What followed was a whirlwind that had this old chaplain in just in awe. Before the words barely cleared the air, Jimmy Lewis handed me $500 as I was walking in the staging lanes.

In the next five hours I was handed fives, tens, twenties, and hundreds by so many people, saying, "Give this to the family." This group from the Temple/Troy area topped $1,700. Big Jim Cole approached me in the winner's circle. "Go pick up my winnings and give it to Cameron." When I got to the tower to collect, I found several other winners checks were donated. The total that day was $11,210. The final amount was between $15,000 and $16,000. Some of the children went out among their own and collected over $30 in coins. The collection also included cards and trinkets to brighten her day.

The conclusion is this: Cameron raced her junior dragster this year. She is cancer free. She is back helping the ladies who teach our children's ministry recruit for kid's church. God is still in the miracle business. God is Good!

PATTIE HEAD

Chaplain Pattie Head with Kid's On Track for Jesus

THERE ARE TIMES in ministry when you feel like you are not making a difference. You begin to get burnt out. You think, "Do I keep going?" I got to that point in Division Nine as Children's Chaplain. I had made up my mind that at the end of the year this is going to be it.

I was at the last race of the year thinking, how am I going to tell everybody this is my last event, that I was going to step back for a while.

All the parents, as they picked up their kids from Chapel Service, began to tell me how thankful they were that I was there. It was like God said, "you are making a difference."

That God would use me to speak at all is amazing. But to speak to kids who took it to their parents and their grandparents was impacting three generations. The parents knew God was working in those children through God Speed Ministry. And that is amazing.

Keith Petersen: GAP Moment Up North

by Division 6 Chaplain Keith Petersen

I ATTEND THE CHRISTIAN & Missionary Alliance Church in Grande Prairie, no not Texas, as the title says, up NORTH! Yes, way up north of the 49th parallel in a small city in Northern Alberta Canada, Grande Prairie. Here at our church, we have a fun way of praising God called GAP moments. GAP stands for, "God Answers Prayer." This is my testimony of how God has answered one of my family's prayers this last year.

Grande Prairie, Alberta is in the booming heart of Canada's oilfield. There are lots of good, well-paying jobs to be had in this part of Canada. I moved here in 2005 after growing up on Vancouver Island, off the coast of British Columbia. Drag racing was bred into me, travelling all around the Northwest with my parents' Super Gas car. I never knew anything other than summers filled with racing, and of course winters filled with good old Canadian hockey, Eh!

Shortly after moving into Grande Prairie, I met my wife at the local dragstrip. Between her, her family, and her family friends, I was led back to Christ as a born-again believer. My wife and I were married in September of 2007. At that time, we decided not to use any birth control and let things happen in God's time. We did not want to try and follow a calendar. We were blessed in January 2009 when our son, Richard Dean, was born. As a family, we decided that one child was enough for the time and went about life as usual.

During that time, the Holy Spirit had gotten hold of me and began to lead me into ministry, at the track, as a Chaplain; a place I never thought I would end up. Once I started submitting to the Spirit, I realized that God wanted me there, and He would show me the way. In 2010, I began to work with God Speed Ministry. The next thing I knew, I was praying with Top Fuel pilots before they went down the track at Castrol Raceway in Edmonton, Alberta. How that happened, God only knows.

In December 2011 we decided it was time to expand our family once again. This time we decided on watching schedules and all the other things that come with trying to get pregnant. We also decided not to tell anyone about what we were doing, so it would be a surprise. Nine months later we still had not succeeded. We both went into the doctor to get checked out. We found that my wife had a few minor things that needed to be straightened out before we would have any success. So, on some pills she went, with an even firmer schedule, and we also began to pray.

Three more months, we still were not pregnant. Two more doses, (six months) of the medication, and still no baby. My wife, who has struggled with depression in the past, was now in a downward spiral that made it hard for her to even get out of bed most mornings.

If you have been keeping up with the months we are now in the early spring of 2013. For you southerners, that's mid-April in Grande Prairie. During the last batch of medication, while my wife lay in bed at home, this testimony was given at church one morning:

Two doctors, husband and wife, had a young daughter who started developing warts all over her body. Mom and Dad being doctors thought, "Easy right, they're just warts, we can fix this." The warts got worse. They went to a specialist. The specialist said, "They're just warts, we can fix this." The warts got worse. After a year and a half of this going on, and multiple doctors pulling their hair out, someone finally said, "Let's pray for her."

The parents brought her into the elders of our church, anointed her with oil and prayed over her. Within weeks, even days, the warts started falling off like scabs. All the warts were gone. Not a mark left on her. That is when GAP moments were born in our church. James 5:14 reads *"Is anyone among you sick? Let him call for the elders of the church, and let them pray over him, anointing him with oil in the name of the Lord."*[8]

I drove home and told my wife all about what I had heard. I said we must do this. A few weeks later, after the last pills had been taken, the elders of Grande Prairie Alliance Church prayed over my wife and me.

Racing season had finally started up in IHRA's Division Six. We were in Ashcroft, British Columbia with my parents. On Saturday we got word that my aunt was losing her battle with cancer. My parents decided to head west, home to Vancouver Island, instead of following us east, out to the Edmonton Nitro Jam. This meant my wife and I now had no place to stay

---

[8]   King James Bible

at the track. We had planned to stay in my parents' trailer, but now a hotel would be our resting place for the weekend.

We are now on the first weekend of July 2013. I do not think I need to get graphic on what the difference is between staying in the back of my parent's trailer and staying in a hotel was. My wife and I had a nice romantic weekend together.

We also had a wonderful weekend at the track with all our friends from IHRA and Renee Bingham from God Speed ministry. We opened up to her about our struggles getting pregnant throughout the weekend, and she made it a point to pray with us. She has been so supportive in my short walk with Christ. She has been such a mentor to me in the ministry that God is developing around the tracks up here in the northwest.

My birthday is on August 6th. My wife took me out to supper at a wonderful steak house. On the way home, she asked me to stop at a pharmacy because she needed to pick something up. I knew she had been not feeling well, so I assumed it was something for the flu bug she had been fighting. We got home from supper and put our son to bed. I proceeded to go about my nightly routine of checking emails and Facebook. That is when my wife gave me the best birthday present I could ever ask for. She came around the corner into the dining room and showed me a pregnancy test that read POSITIVE. We were excited to say the least. I praised God and knew this was Him. Then she told me that if her math was correct, it happened in Edmonton.

My aunt lost her battle with cancer and went to be with the Lord the Tuesday after the race in Edmonton. So, it was a good thing my parents had decided to head home instead of going to the next race. My aunt was an amazing woman. She was all about blessing others, making sure others were taken care of before herself. I believe, that even in death she would have wanted someone to receive a blessing out of it. She got her wish. Through death God brought life. That is my GAP moment.

My victories at the track are no longer defined by round wins. They are more defined by the relationships that are being sown, and the seeds that are being planted to further God's kingdom. As for me, and my house (my growing family), we will serve the Lord. Amen.

Jesus the Great Physician

By Deborah Tankersley

Joe and I are in Florida for the division race and the NHRA Gator National event. His Lenco broke Saturday and some friends recommended a shop to fix it. When we got there and unloaded it Joe came back out and said the guy and his wife had something to show me. I am thinking pet??? Pontiac???.

So, we go in and they lead me to the side of the refrigerator where I see two index cards with a Band-Aid and a Bible verse. I recognize this as a lesson that I had shared with my daughter Laurel's help, maybe fifteen years ago. Their girls are grown now, they have moved but the index cards are still on the fridge.

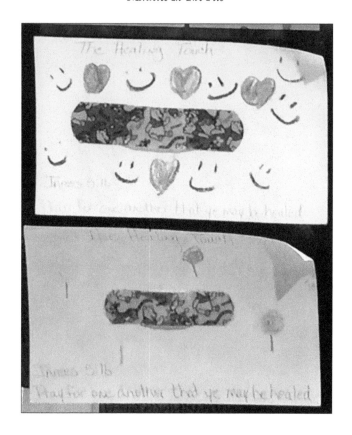

Jesus the Great Physician index cards

Then they tell me this lesson, **Jesus the Great Physician**, I called it, was a life changer for their family. The Granddad had cancer with only a year to live. They prayed and claimed healing for him. He and one of the girls were saved and baptized the same day! He did go on to be with the Lord, but they had the joy of knowing that he had not only ultimate healing but life everlasting.

What an awesome God that allowed us to know the rest of that story. All I could do was stand there with tears rolling down my face.

Love y'all Deborah Tankersley

MATT COLLIER-
MY CANCER STORY

SEVENTEEN YEARS AGO, I chose to become a Christian, not because I thought that I was perfect, because I knew I was not. I wanted to follow the One who is. However, that does not mean that I always get it right. I became a Christian.

I began to hear God's voice like his real voice as clear as one person talking to another. You think that that would startle someone, but His voice is so comforting. His voice is backed by His promise. That is when I choose to listen to it.

You see, there have been times when I told him what I was going to do despite what He had said. And like a loving father He took me back when I went astray. Every single time.

I heard His voice when He told me to work at the high school where I teach.

I heard His voice when He told me I would marry my wife, on our first date. Of course, I waited to tell her until later in the relationship.

I heard His voice before I would pray with my high school soccer players before and after each game.

February 2019, I was certain I had pneumonia and walked into urgent care. I expected to walk out with a prescription for an antibiotic and be done. Instead, I walked out with a mass in my chest about the size of a softball. Further scans would show I had tumors on my pancreas, my kidneys, and my liver. T-cell Lymphoblastic Lymphoma. Stage III.

I did not get to hear the news with my wife beside me. Instead, three former students, now nurses, surrounded me. And we all cried.

That night in the hospital bed I had come to terms with my diagnosis and prayed that my family would be looked after. When God answered He said, "It is finished." It took me a minute to realize He did not say I was finished. He said, "It is finished." I realized my story was not done.

Honest confession. For about a year before my diagnosis I felt like what I had been doing did not matter. I thought I was not a good enough husband, father, teacher. I had been looking for other jobs and opportunities right up to the point I walked into Urgent Care. I was often angry and frustrated. I did not hear God's voice, because I was not listening to it.

Over the course of the next year, I underwent five rounds of chemotherapy, five blood transfusions, six lumbar punctures for bone marrow biopsies, a bone marrow transplant, had pneumonia three times, received fifteen localized radiation treatments; then underwent double hernia surgery.

I prayed that my healing would bring glory to God. I prayed to be His miracle. I told the doctors they were going to be part of something amazing. I shared my faith with the nurses, the doctors, radiologists, other patients, friends, students, and family.

After a long recovery at home, in November, my scans showed I was cancer free.

I continued to share my story. His story.

February has often been a momentous month for me over my lifetime.

I got my first dog.

I met my wife.

I was baptized as an adult.

And I was diagnosed with cancer all during the month of February.

February 2020, I had another PET scan, but this time I was scared. I feared the worst.

Last night, my doctor called and said he was eighty to ninety percent sure the cancer had returned.

I dropped to my knees and I cried. Then I yelled at God and told him He lied. You said it was finished.

Two days later, we met with a pulmonologist who reviewed my scans and said he was eighty to ninety percent sure it was not cancer.

Two different diagnoses. Who was I supposed to trust? Who was I supposed to believe? Who was I supposed to listen to?

The pulmonologist scheduled a procedure a few days later. After the procedure, when I was coming out of anesthesia, a nurse revived me slowly. She said my wife would be in to see me shortly. And to rest while she went to finish with another patient. She left.

I closed my eyes. I felt someone embrace me from the side and say, "I told you you'd be alright." I smiled and opened my eyes. No one was there. You see, God never took back as promised. He never left me. In fact, He held me even closer.

The results were conclusive. No cancer.

What happened was that I had chosen to listen to man. I became too comfortable and stopped listening. I told you I did not always get it right. I also told you God takes you back when you go astray.

I am quite sure my guardian angel has continuously put his face in his palm and asked, "really, this guy." Jesus always replied, "Yes, especially him."

And he says that about you as well. He will always go after His lost sheep.

Cancer is an ugly evil. It does not care how old you are. How young you are. How much money you have. What religion you are. What occupation you have. What race you are. It does not care if you are a mother, a father, a son, a daughter, grandmother, grandfather.

Cancer comes in many forms. It is not just in debilitating tumors and masses. It takes shape in "I can't do this," "I am not smart enough," "I will never be able to," "If only I had what he had." These cancers fester when we follow the ways in the world.

Look around you now. Who are you listening to? There is plenty of noise in social media, news broadcasts, and everyone's opinion. But I promise God is talking. We need to be still. Miracles do not look the same now as they did during Jesus's time. But I assure you they happen every day.

God did not give me cancer, but He used it to show how powerful He is. He is using it for me, a flawed and imperfect person to share his story.

I am asking, "Have you heard Him?"

Are you listening?

MATT COLLIER- REFLECTIONS

IN OUR HOUSE, we discuss the gifts that God has given us, how we are unique, and how we can use them to honor Him and tell people about Jesus. We call them our superpowers. My daughter Everleigh can see things in her dreams play out in life later. My daughter Ailey hears God's voice when she talks to Him. My wife Lisa feels God's presence when she makes decisions. I have an exceptional sense of humor! (My girls would tell you that is not remotely true.)

Before I chose to become a Christian, I belonged to the church of good. Do you know what I mean? If my actions were good, I would be considered for heaven. I did not talk to God unless I needed something that would surely benefit me. It was more like wishing on a star rather than a close relationship.

When I surrendered my life to Christ, all that changed. I wanted to do things that would glorify Him. I wanted to be in constant prayer about how my life changed because I followed Him. What I am saying is I did not become a Christian because I thought I would be perfect; it was because I knew I was not, and I wanted a relationship with the One who is!

Recently I told my girls about something I experienced a few months after I became a Christian in 2003. I told them I got into bed at 10:00 pm and closed my eyes. When I did, I saw myself opening the door to my apartment with my dog. I walked down the steps and out into the grass covered area of the complex. The morning sun was shining so brightly. Birds were chirping. Flowers and trees were everywhere in vibrant colors and had the most beautiful aroma. I looked down at my dog and saw she was wagging her tail in delight.

There were several of my neighbors out as well soaking in that moment. Then I heard a terrible shriek. People began screaming and pointing to the sky in the distance. Someone shouted, "it's the end of the world!"

I could see it begin to change from a brilliant blue to a deep red like spilled watercolor on a canvas. In front of the red was a line of black, which as it spread and came closer, I could see that it was made of black birds. The line of birds came closer, changing the horizon. As they appeared directly over my head, they all came together and took the shape of a man in a robe.

As soon as I could make out that it was Jesus, I began an ascent straight up, following the flight of birds higher and higher. As I ascended, I could barely breathe, much like when you jump from a hot tub into a cold swimming pool and try to catch your breath. I could hear the loud rush of air passing over me as it made my eyes tear up and blink. Then suddenly I stopped. I was floating. It was completely silent.

As I looked around me, I could not see my body, arms, or legs. I looked out into the distance and could see what I thought was land but was a shoreline of clouds with a sunrise behind it. I saw a wide line of people of all ages and nationalities approaching the edge. It was several rows deep. These people looked so familiar. I know I knew them, yet I could not think of their names or exactly why they were so familiar. They stopped at the edge. As they looked out at me, they smiled and nodded slowly. I started to feel warm, but I had no body.

I opened my eyes and was gasping for breath. The clock still showed 10:00pm.

The next morning, I walked out of my apartment and down the stairs with my dog and peered out apprehensively at the landscape and then turned my eyes to the sky searching all over.

I have not told many people about this experience when I told my children the other night. The first thing they said was, "But dad, you were born without a sense of smell! How did you smell all the flowers?" It is something that I can never describe to people because I have nothing to compare it to. All I know is that I can still "smell it."

After I shared all of this, they then asked what it meant. A few pastors have told me that it means I am saved and it is a Rapture experience. However, I always knew there was something more. Who were all those people and why did I know them?

Up until that moment I told my daughters, I had absolutely no idea what it meant. Then in that instance it came to me; God was telling me that yes, I was saved, but that I had a purpose. That purpose was to be a light for others. His light. All those people I saw on the cloud shoreline were people I had witnessed to over my lifetime. People who came to know Christ because Christ was in me. Because they had heard about how Christ changed me and would change them. God was showing me the impact I would have for His Kingdom.

I wear a shirt designed and sold by my Journalism students to help support my family when I was diagnosed with cancer over two years ago. It is based on my fondness for Superman, my love for writing, and my faith. It says, "The story is written." They knew I was not done, and that God would work through me. Even though the giant "C" was meant to represent my last name Collier, to me it really means Christ. His story is written. I may admire the Man of Steel who can stop bullets, but I was truly saved by the man who took three nails and all the world's sin for me.

Remember I said I am not perfect. Even after my salvation, I have said and done things I should not have. I have looked at things I should not have. I have thought about things I should not have. I fail every day. But I am also redeemed every day. God can use anything, even our imperfections to glorify Him. Are you struggling with addictions? Are you struggling with your relationships? Do you feel like you are not good enough to be loved by

Jesus? Are you running from Him? Christ will always come after you and bring you home.

Don't believe me?

Elijah – Was suicidal.

Joseph – Was abused.

Moses – Had a speech problem.

Gideon – Was afraid.

Rahab – Was a prostitute.

Noah – Was Drunk.

Jeremiah – Was young.

Jacob – Was a cheater.

David – Was a murderer.

Jonah – Ran from God.

Naomi – Was a widow.

Peter – Denied Christ three times.

Martha – Worried about everything.

The Disciples – Fell asleep while praying.

Paul – A Pharisee persecuted Christians before becoming one.

Matt Collier–was born without a sense of smell and dry sense of humor.

Are you ready to find out what your superpower is? Are you ready to use it to glorify Him?

Are you ready to stop running from Him?

Cameron Choate, Sean Clevenger, Donnie Crowder
By Renee Bingham

I HAVE HAD MANY moments when death and destruction have tried our faith and tested our belief and reliance upon the word of God. Like Elijah I have stood against the rain when it threatened to cancel God ordained plans. I have seen God part the clouds and create a hole around the racetracks as I have watched on live radar. Not only have I witnessed this, but other chaplains have been threatened with rain during their services in the grandstands only to see God stop the rain until the service was over. Many IHRA officials and racers have witnessed the miracles God has performed in weather situations.

I have seen God give life back to three individuals who had absolutely no hope.

CAMERON CHOATE WED, MAY 30, 2006
Please pray for Cameron Choate, five-year-old daughter of Scooter & Jamie Choate, Division 4 Quick Rod racers, (Jamie also helps Sylvia Maedgen with the God Speed Children's ministry.) Cameron is in ICU at Fort Worth Children's Hospital. They have done surgery to remove an infection. She is one sick little girl and needs our prayers.

This was the prayer request that came for Cameron Choate. A spider had bitten her. Her life was in danger.

The doctors told the Choates that there was nothing more they could do for their daughter after dozens of surgeries and 5 weeks in intensive care. Cameron would be dead later that day. But God heard the prayers of the multitudes praying for her. Cameron survived the spider bite thanks to God.

In treating her for the spider bite, they discovered she had leukemia. It appeared the bad had just gotten worse.

God worked miracle after miracle in Cameron's life. The racing community supported Scotter & Jamie like drag racers do. Prayers, money, visits, help, and more prayers until the word came, "Cameron is in remission!"

Today Cameron is still cancer free and a beautiful, healthy, young lady. Thank you, God!

SEAN CLEVENGER

Sean Clevenger was a dead man when he arrived at the hospital. They put him on life support until his parents arrived. It was medically impossible for him to survive. Did they want to donate his organs? Again, God heard the prayers of those racers raised up in answer to our prayers. Sean is alive and praising God, and the doctors are testifying of the miracle.

DONNIE CROWDER

Donnie Crowder was given less than six weeks to live because of an inoperable tumor in January of 2005. By May he was cancer free and back working at the racetrack.

Chapter 4

TESTIMONIES OF THE RACERS GOD SPEED MINISTRY SERVES

Daily Wisdom from Casey Davis

Dear Renee and Lisa,

THIS MESSAGE HIT just at the right time. I know you two are busy women and you know what God is capable of, but I feel I must share why this message is so important to me.

This past Monday my house payment was due, along with insurance and the rest of my utilities. Upon updating my checkbook, I did not even have enough money to pay for my house payment, let alone everything else. I was scrambling for cash, (including looking in couch cushions for change).

So, since everything was shut down Monday for the 4th of July, I had to take care of it on Tuesday. By that time, I thought I had gathered enough to barely get by. I had filled an entire thirty two ounce cup full of change, which usually brings about $80.

On my way to the bank with my change I came to a stop light where there were people asking for change for an International Church for feeding the needy, (or something of that nature, the light turned green, and I didn't get a chance to talk to them much). I grabbed all the change in my pocket and some out of the cup and threw it in the bucket. As I got about one hundred yards away something hit me. I made an immediate U turn (legally) and went back to the same guy. I emptied my cup into his bucket. I knew God was there and He would take care of me no matter what. He was the only way I was going to be able to get my bills paid.

The next day I sold a truck that I had been trying to sell for weeks. It was enough to pay for all my bills and give me a little cushion. Since then, I have been getting all sorts of attention on the things I have been trying to sell. I can only say it happened because of God, and what your message had to say nailed it on the head! I hope that made sense! It was a quick version! Hope all is well in North Carolina! God Bless, Casey Davis

ANGELS LINE THE TRACK

Renee Bingham

I WAS WORKING AT the IHRA team finals at Rockingham Dragway in North Carolina. It was time to do the pre-race ceremonies. I stood beside Scott Heaton, the announcer, to do the invocation. As I prayed, I asked the angels to literally line the facility to keep the racers safe and to speed them on their way.

When I finished praying, I turned to hand the microphone back to Scott for the national anthem. But Scott was acting strange. In fact, I was afraid he was having a seizure as he was shaking so violently.

After the national anthem, Scott turned to me and said, "Did you feel them? They flew through here so fast they almost knocked me over."

"Scott, what are you talking about?" I asked.

He replied, " When you called for the angels to line this facility, they flew through here so quickly to take their place along the track that they almost knocked me over. Wow! The angels are lining this track today."

God loves to answer our prayers!

Bobby Hicks
Testimony/Challenge

Bobby Hicks is a retired police officer. Now he is the truck driver for the Aruba Pro Stock drag racing team. This is how God used him, a good ole southern boy, to touch the lives of desperate people.

MY NAME IS Bobby Hicks. I am with Team Aruba. I feel like God has blessed me more than I deserve. As a child I never knew the love of a mom and daddy. From the time I was eight years old until now, I have lived by myself. I raised myself. My grandmother did everything she could for me. She was a third shift worker in a textile plant. She had to do what she had to do.

But not to dwell much on that, the Lord has blessed me.

I had a terrible childhood. I have been molested. I have been beat. My daddy tried to cut my throat. You name it, it has happened to me.

But God has blessed me.

I had a terrible childhood but let me tell you about my adulthood.

I met an angel. I was twelve and she was ten. We went through school together. We have been married for thirty-seven years. I have two of the greatest daughters anyone could ever ask for. I have three grandchildren.

Let me tell you something about grandchildren. Everyone knows that 'theirs are the purdiest'. Everybody knows that they have the best grandchildren that there are. And nobody argues about it. Everybody just knows it. Ain't that great?!

I was a police officer for twenty-five years. In those twenty-five years, I have seen people burned up. I have seen people in car wrecks who begged to be shot.

You may have heard of the Susan Smith incident where the mother drowned her own two children. I was the police officer on that call. I got Michael and Alex out of the back seat of that car. Two babies.

But the worst thing that ever happened to me in my career was this. We got a call, my partner and I, to come to a house where someone was trying to get into a house with a rifle to kill people.

If you have ever been in law enforcement or know anything about law enforcement, you know you get these calls. It is not a big deal. People see things in the middle of the night, but we must check.

We pulled up in the front yard and the first thing we see is a man running off the front porch with a M16 rifle. He had four magazines full, thirty-two round clips. He meant business. He was sixteen years old.

I talked to him. We all got triangled; two officers on each side of the house, my partner with me as I talked to him, asking him what was going on. No matter what I said, he had a comeback.

I told him he did not want to do this to his family. "My family don't care. They run me off."

This young man had intentions of killing other people. But in a flash, he whipped that barrel around and stuck in in his mouth.

I said, "Son, please don't! Wait! Let me at least pray for you."

This haunts me to this very day. He said, "Sir, don't you think it's a little late." He pulls the trigger. He's gone.

People, let me tell you. The young people walking around this racetrack, you do not know what is going on in their head. You do not know what they are thinking about. You do not know what is on their mind. I do not care if he is the one that has his breaches hanging down past his hiney. I do not care if he has tattoos everywhere. I do not care if he looks like he fell in a tackle box. Someone needs to love that young man. Someone needs to love that young girl. And I know today, that if you walk up and just hug a young girl, someone will say, "he's some kind of pervert." I do not care!

If I see a young person, I walk up to them, put my arm around them and say, "I LOVE YOU! My God loves you!"

And if it embarrasses you, something is wrong with you.

Reach in your pocket. Pull out a piece of paper and a pen. Print your name on it. Give it to that young person. "If you EVER need someone to talk to, this is my number." You will be surprised what it means to those young people.

If us Christians cannot do it, if we are the ones who love the Lord, and we cannot do it, who is going to do it? O.... does not care. Any of the big stars do not care. It is up to us to care. We are the church. It is up to us to commit to telling a young person you love them.

Walk up to them. Put your arm around them. Tell them you love them. Tell them God loves them. Go the straight path.

Bobby shared this testimony at the IHRA Spring Nationals at Rockingham Dragway.

SEEK AND YOU WILL FIND

by Van Abernethy

And you will seek Me and find Me when you search for Me
with all your heart. Jeremiah 29:13 (NKJV)[9]

THAT PASSAGE IN Jeremiah is a favorite of my dad's because it so reminds him of his salvation experience. My dad was saved when he was around thirty-five. He had hit his own personal rock bottom, which is what it takes to get some people's attention. The day my dad found the Lord (or perhaps the day the Lord found my dad) he was driving his worn-out Jeep Scout up a mountain after a horrendous downpour. My dad's intent was to get alone and do business with God, and nothing was going to stop him.

He got his Jeep stuck in the mud, so he walked the rest of the way. Once he crested the top of the mountain my dad began gathering stones to make

---

himself an altar at which to pray. He read in the Old Testament they used to do that so he figured he should do it too. So, there he was, covered in mud, kneeling at the foot of a pile of stones as he cried out to Jesus to be his Savior. In other words, he was "seeking God with all his heart"...and believe me when I say he found Him.

God no doubt has pity on such brokenness and humility. My dad had a four pack a day cigarette habit when he climbed that mountain that day. He laid his last pack on top of his stone altar and God delivered him from smoking that day. My dad has never smoked another one since. My dad loved beer as well, and although he did not have one handy to lay on his altar, the Lord took that desire away as well.

Now sixty-four years old, the life-changing power of Christ that took place all those years ago on top of that mountain is still alive and well in my dad's life. He went from a broken, muddy sinner to a Sunday School teacher and strong man of God. Only Jesus can make such a difference.

Where Do You Find a Christian

By Marie Waller

A MAN RUSHED INTO The Inn, a Christian coffee shop in Salisbury, North Carolina one Saturday night. He excitedly searched for Tom, the owner. It was the coffee shop's anniversary, and the place was packed with live music and celebrating supporters. Someone pointed the searching man in Tom's direction. The man rushed over to Tom and said, "I did not know where to find Christians on a Saturday night, but I knew you would be here. Please tell me how to be saved. I must be saved." Tom led the man to salvation that night.

Who else might be looking for Christians on a Saturday night? One of our friends, neighbors, or coworkers, perhaps? Will they know where to find us? Can they tell who we are as we race, work, and play?

We are all on a search for Christ. God has placed a desire for Himself within the heart of every person. Everyone you meet is in some way either searching for God or denying their heart's desire for Him. Will they know where to find you or even know to look for you when they are ready to ask Christ to be Lord of their lives? Where are you on a Saturday night? Where are your Christian friends and family? Are you visible? Are you a city on a hill? Or do you look so much like the world that someone searching for a Christian would not come looking for you?

We are called to be the light of the world. The salt of the earth. The aroma of Christ. Set apart. Holy.

Are Christians only to be seen on Sunday mornings? Are they only to fellowship together at Church meetings? How would you answer the question: "Where do you find a Christian on a Saturday night?"

True story told by Marie Waller

An 'Official' Miracle -The Sam Kearns Story

On Thursday, May 26th, 2011, IHRA Official, Sam Kearns, was rushed to the hospital with paralysis and a suspected stroke. However, the diagnosis turned out to be much worse. The paralysis was caused by four large tumors in his brain. The tumors were pushing Sam's brain off-center and crushing it against the left side of his skull, thus causing the paralysis and other issues.

Surgery proved to be futile as the tumors were larger and more invasive than expected, making them inoperable. The staff of McLeod Medical Center diagnosed Sam with rare, but treatable brain cancer, Non-Hodgkins Lymphoma.

Thus began a roller coaster of events for Sam and his close friend, Wanda. Sam had no insurance. It was a battle to even gain the intense chemo treatment needed. Racers poured forth their kindness with calls, cards, and even monetary donations. They gave $2,609.00 to help with Sam's medical bills and expenses. Thankfully, Sam was approved for financial aid and the treatment began.

Sam's doctor began a barrage of five different chemotherapies to attack the massive tumors. The chemo cocktails were so severe they required an antidote within twenty-four hours or the treatment itself would kill Sam. Sam continued to battle with the intense treatments, bouts of depression and mounting medical bills for a month.

Then, on June 21st the doctors wanted to run another MRI to assess the tumor's growth rate. What they found instead was a miracle: NO TUMORS!

Word spread quickly of the miracle and people everywhere rejoiced in God's goodness.

As a precaution, the doctors continued treatment and did another scan on July 12th. The text came in from Wanda: "Drum roll please!!!! Still no tumors!!!!!!!!!!!!!"

The Lord healed Sam of all brain tumors and restored complete function to his body! Our God is a miracle-working God who is bigger than brain tumors, divorce, disease, and despair. He bends low to listen to us and searches the earth to bless us. He may not always answer our prayers with an "official" miracle, but He will always accomplish His best for our good and His glory.

In the words of Wanda, "Do not ever give up. Do not ever give up. God still moves mountains!"

THANK YOU, GOD SPEED

I WOULD LIKE TO thank you and the ministry that you bring to the racetrack. I would just like to tell you how great Tammie (Smith) is. When I was at the PDRA event at GALOT Motorsports Park, I was at the lowest point in my life and ready to end it all. She, out of the blue, walks up to me like she knew something was wrong. We talked and she said a prayer with me. She may not know it, but she saved my life that day. Thank You for all you and your crew bring to the track. From Steve Bowen 11.10.22

***

Thursday, June 14, 2007, 5:23 PM An email to IHRA from a spectator.

Recently, my husband and I attended the Sooner Nationals in Tulsa, Oklahoma. It was the first major racing event I had ever been to, and I am thirty-nine. I am hooked, and we are making plans to attend future events!!!

The reason for my email is to say THANK YOU and BLESS YOU. I am not sure if you are the person this mail needs to be directed to but thought I would be off to a good start by sending it to you. At the beginning of the race we attended, a prayer was said asking the Lord for safety, health and to bless everyone at the race. In this day and age, my husband and I both were surprised and very moved to see that prayer was still held at such a public event. We have watched prayer be kicked out of our schools and sporting events, the Ten Commandments removed from our courthouses and watch the collapse of belief in general. It was very moving to see that a sport as big as the IHRA feels there is both a need and a desire to have prayer before beginning events. You and those involved in keeping prayer alive will be rewarded by our Heavenly Father. My husband and I thank you and will continue to pray for the sport of drag racing. Bless you, Ted and Suzanne Hunt, Chelsea, Oklahoma

GREG'S STORY

ON WEDNESDAY, SEPT. 17th, Greg Slack was diagnosed with Mantle Cell Lymphoma, an exceedingly rare form of cancer. His doctor explained it this way. "Greg, if someone told you that you were going to have lymphoma – no way around it – but you get to choose which one, this would not be the one you would choose. It is mean, it is ugly, and it is aggressive. The survival rate is zero."

Later that evening, Gina, Greg's wife, called God Speed Ministry, asking us to contact the prayer warriors on Greg's behalf. They needed all the prayer they could get as they began this journey into the unknown. The request went out across the United States and Canada late that night.

Thursday morning, Greg and Gina's cell phones began ringing. People called to pray with Greg and promised him to continue to pray for him. Someone in Kentucky, whom Greg had only met once, called to pray, and pray powerfully. So, it continued. So many people called on Thursday and Friday that Greg had to charge his phone twice during the day. People stopped by Greg's business to show their support by their presence, and by their tears.

As Gina said, "The best thing about this week is all the love and support we have received from so many people. It is unbelievable. We know a lot of people but we had no idea so many knew us and would care enough to call. It is truly remarkable."

On Saturday morning, Greg was taking his customary walk across his yard to his parents' home for their standing breakfast date. He felt exceptionally good, even better than his best days before being diagnosed with cancer. As he was walking, he sensed God's presence with him very strongly.

In his spirit, he heard God's voice: "Greg, do you have any idea how many prayers I have heard on your behalf since Wednesday night?" Wow! Greg's spirit soared. As Gina said, "He is singing like a canary. He cannot stop singing."

At breakfast Sunday morning, Greg's mother, whose health is declining, was determined to go to church with Greg and Gina. When Gina asked Greg's dad if he wanted to go with them, instead of his usual quick "no" (he does not attend church), he simply said "I don't think so."

At church, most had not heard of Greg's diagnosis. Their Sunday School class discarded their lesson to pray and cry with Greg and Gina. As Gina left the classroom to go to the Worship Service, she saw Greg's mother and father standing in the back. She quickly turned back to tell Greg, "Your dad is here!" It was an answer to years of prayer.

During the prayer request time, Greg shared his diagnosis with the congregation. "I do not know what the future holds. But I do know that if the Lord Jesus were to walk in the back door and say, 'Come on Greg, it's time to go.' I would say, 'Okay Lord, just a moment.' Then I would turn to Gina to tell her bye, 'I love you. I will see you when you get to heaven. Just do not be too long.'"

"None of us know when it is our time to die. We must be ready. I am ready. We all need to live each moment as if it were our last. Are you ready?"

P.S. Greg is still alive. He is past the five year mark. God worked greatly in his life.

Greg & Gina Slack's story told by Gina to Renee Bingham

Jim Wood's Testimony

LONG STORY SHORT, I should not even be here.

I drive a semi-truck carrying hazmat, hydra ammonia, extremely dangerous. I was going to North Carolina. I was on the turnpike in West Virginia. I started feeling bad. I was trying to get off the mountain before anything happened with the truck. I made it to the Virginia Welcome Center. Someone called 911. They took me from there to a hospital. I had a stroke.

They took me back home to Ohio. I was in three or four different hospitals. They could not find out what happened, what caused it. Finally, they got me to the University of Cincinnati in Ohio. They found it there. It is an advanced hospital.

This is how they explained it. You have two carotid arteries here (pointing to either side of his neck) and two in the back going to the center of your brain. I had a blockage and a blood clot on my brain stem and another blood clot on my brain. They were going to operate on me three separate times. And they could not do it. They said when they got to the first clot and break the stuff up, it goes through the arteries. It would kill me before they could get to the second one.

They gave me zero chance if I had the operation. But if I did not have the operation, they gave me zero chance. The odds were not particularly good. But we had faith. Everybody was praying, keeping me in their thoughts and prayers.

Connie, my wife, was on day five of this ordeal. They said, "We are going to operate on you." It was the fourth time they said it. They said, "We don't have any choice."

To show you how serious it was, I did my last will and testament in the room with Connie, and had it notarized. My dad and I made the funeral arrangements because the doctors said my chances were zero; I was not going to come back out. I never gave up. I stayed in faith. We prayed all the time. I kept my faith. I knew people were praying.

They called up to say they were coming to get me in a few minutes. I was saying goodbye to Connie. That was the hardest part. I was okay with the dying part. I had peace with God, and I knew where I was going. But that was the hardest part.

We were sitting there. I had a team of ten doctors. We were waiting for them to come in to get me. This doctor came in. I never caught his name. I had never seen him before. He came in and sat down. He said, "I want to talk to you and your wife about what is about to happen."

I said, "I pretty well know what is about to happen. I am ready."

We sat there. He talked to us for about ten to fifteen minutes. Right out of the clear blue, he said, "I'm going to cancel the operation."

We looked at each other, then said, "why?"

He said, "I've got an idea. I want to do a combination of drugs and double dose it. I want to give that to you. Maybe we can burn that clot away. It has never been done before."

At least I had an option. I said, "Okay."

As he left, he said, "All the surgeons are in a meeting right now, deciding how they are going to do the operation." He left.

In came one of the surgeons we had been talking to all along. He said, "We were in a meeting, and we have an idea. We are going to try a combination of drugs and double dose you to try to burn it away."

I said, "That's what that other doctor said."

He said, "There was no other doctor from here."

I turned to the nurse and asked her the name of the doctor who was in there. She said no doctor has been in here.

I knew I was going to be okay.

I have to back up.

When I had the second stroke, they took me to Coldwater Hospital which was one-hundred-thirty miles from Cincinnati. They sent their helicopter to get me and bring me back. They took me straight to intensive care.

All this story took place in intensive care. But after this experience with the doctor and the team of doctors having the idea, I walked out of intensive care and out of the hospital. I went from a zero chance of living to home.

God had his angel right there if it was not Him Himself!

We never gave up. All the thoughts and prayers...I get very emotional. I was ready for the dying part. I was at peace. My hardest part was leaving Connie behind. I was more worried about her than I was about me. But I know. I know where I am going. I know where she is going. We will all see each other in heaven.

I want to back up one more time.

When that happened in August, and they sent me home, about 3:00 a.m. I got up to go to the bathroom. We had just bought a place in the country in Ohio. I went to the restroom. When I came back, the curtain of one of the two windows was open a few inches.

When I took two steps into the bedroom, the brightest light... If you can imagine the brilliant light of a transformer when it blows out, multiply that by ten-thousand.... came through the window and hit me in the chest.

I woke Connie up and said, "I think we blew a transformer. Now wait a minute, we live in the country. We do not have a transformer." I even went outside looking. I looked all over. There was nothing.

This came from heaven. I knew something was going to happen. With our faith and with our health, here I am. I went from zero to one hundred. And I was racing yesterday.

Jim Woods and his wife Connie worked as officials for IHRA. He also races the Stock/Super Stock classes. Jim shared this testimony at the IHRA Pro Am event at Immokalee Regional Raceway in Immokalee, Florida.

LEVI'S ENCOUNTER WITH HOLY SPIRIT AND ANGELS

I HAVE HAD SPIRITUAL encounters but nothing like my daughter and fourteen-year-old grandson recently experienced. Here is their story. – Renee Bingham

It is a new, small home church in central Ohio started by my daughter Christy and son-in-law Landon. They meet in a barn on their property. Previously, they only attended traditional denominational churches: Methodist and Nazarene. They had no experience like the one about to happen.

June 10, 2018, started like a normal Sunday evening service with worship and a sermon. At the end of the message, they had a time of prayer where two elders prayed over Christy and Landon. They anointed them as leaders of the church. Afterwards, they invited others to come up for prayer if they wanted.

Several people came up for prayer, but it was when Levi, Christy's son, came up for prayer, that the Holy Spirit really became evident. After praying for him, Christy took anointing oil and anointed the tops of Levi's feet. He fell on the floor under the power of the Holy Spirit. After laying there for a few seconds they helped him into a chair where he sat savoring God's Presence.

Prayer time continued with several other people coming up to receive prayer. Before prayer time concluded Levi came back, "I want more," he said. He asked for more prayer and more anointing oil. As they prayed for him, he was experiencing some sort of breakthrough or freedom.

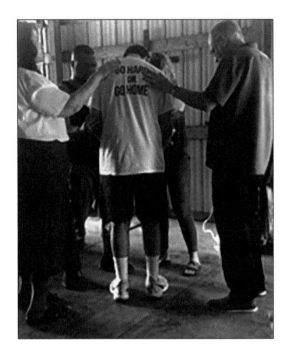

People praying over Levi

As the prayer concluded, Christy anointed his ears, and once again he fell on the floor overwhelmed by the Holy Spirit. As he lay on the floor he asked for a pen and paper. He started to write prophecies for the church and for the people.

When he was finally able to stand (with help), he started sharing the prophecies God had given him. Lavonne, one of the elders, helped read the prophecies as he was sobbing under the power of the Spirit.

However, there was one lady, Becky, for whom Levi did not have a prophecy. He asked the women of the church to circle her to pray. After praying for a few minutes, Levi, still under the influence of the Spirit, told Becky to go outside and stand in a specific spot. He asked the women to come around and continue praying for her. As the women prayed for Becky, Levi continued to write prophecy and direction for the church.

Levi showing Becky where to stand

Then he gave Becky specific instructions, on paper, of how to pray for her husband, who had left her and was addicted to drugs. But before she could effectively pray for her husband, she had to have peace. Becky was distraught because she felt no peace. As the women continued to pray, God was able to restore Becky's peace and joy.

Levi came over and said a demon would leave Becky. He said, "I get to see it leave. Someone else will too."

After instructing Becky to burn the piece of paper with the instructions to pray for her husband, Levi saw the demon come out of her.

God touched this ordinary church for ninety minutes. Levi, just fourteen years old, was leading and directing as he followed God. People's lives were changed forever that night.

After the service, Christy talked to Levi. "What made you come up for prayer?" Levi said, "I wanted in the gold circle around you."

"What?"

"Yes, there was a gold circle around the four of you as Lavonne and Eric prayed for you and Landon."

Levi asked if other people had seen all the angels in the church that night. He said there were at least six, maybe eight angels. He said it was hard to tell how many because of how bright they were. Then he said, "There was this really big angel standing outside. I knew Becky needed to be near him. That is why I took her outside to pray in that particular spot. I wanted her to be near him."

"What was it like for you during all this?"

"I could feel what people were feeling: some were confused, some in disbelief, some felt joy. Somehow, I knew I would not remember much of what happened. I got to see Matt (who has cerebral palsy and has a disfigured arm and leg) in heaven. He was completely whole and healed. I felt the love of God so strong. I know more than anything else, God wants to heal people and it IS possible here on earth."

Christy said the next day Levi had little memory of what all happened and was just Levi, playing ball, lifting weights, and teasing his younger brother.

HEALED HANDS

FEBRUARY 7, 2015: It was a beautiful Saturday in Tucson, Arizona where Michael Hunt and his son Ren were getting ready to race at the IHRA Southwestern National Event. When they cranked the car, it backfired through the carburetor. Michael's shirt caught fire. In trying to get it off, both hands became wrapped in it and burned. His son Ren reached in to rip it off him and received burns of a lesser degree.

Michael was airlifted to the hospital. Miraculously he was released later that day. He returned to the track with both hands completely bandaged. He was extremely grateful for all the prayers from the God Speed Ministry team.

March 22, 2015 "Look! Look!" Michael Hunt stopped Renee Bingham at the PDRA Texas Nationals at the Texas Motorplex. "Look at my hands." He wiggled all his fingers and proudly displayed his healed hands. "Thank you and thank God. Thank God for how well I am healed."

Together we celebrated God's goodness and miraculous healing power. God loves to include us in His work and blessings. Thank all who prayed.

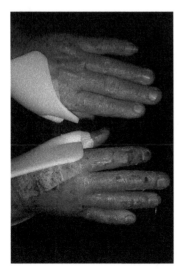 

God's Mighty Hand

By Bruce Thrift, Gary & Renee Bingham

Bruce Thrift, Top Sportsman racer, called Gary Bingham on Monday with a prayer request. His foreman for Thrift Roofing, Jeremy, was in a tough situation. On Sunday October 16, 2016, Jeremy found his 2-year-old floating face down in the middle of a pond. An older sibling and the two-year-old were out playing and managed to get through the boundaries of the neighbor's property where there was a pond. The two-year-old fell in. His brother ran to get help. That is where Jeremy found his son's body. They began CPR. He was taken to the hospital and put on life support.

Monday, October 17, 2016: The child's brain was swelling. The doctors told the family there was no hope. They wanted to remove him from life support around 2 p.m. They gave the family time to say goodbye. That was when Bruce Thrift called for prayer. The prayer request went out from God Speed Ministry across the world for people to pray for God to spare this child's life.

Tuesday, October 18, 2016, 7:30 a.m.: He lives! The report came that he was breathing on his own. The family was rejoicing. The doctors cautioned about brain damage. They predicted a dire future for the child if he did continue to live. Again, Bruce asked God Speed Ministry for prayer for the little boy to be okay. The request went out and people prayed.

At 7:00 pm the report came, "the child is up running around the hospital, playing. The doctors are considering sending him home tomorrow!!!! Praise God!"

Wednesday, October 19, 2016: The doctors released the little boy who was one-hundred percent. The family stopped at McDonald's on the way home to celebrate and play.

What a mighty, awesome, good, good God we serve. Thank you, God. Thank you, prayer warriors for interceding. God's mighty hand raised and restored this child.

Here are some responses from the prayer warriors:

J.M. Wow! Wow! Wow! What an awesome God we serve!

D.T. Thank you so much for the updates. I had been praying for him again this morning and was contemplating emailing you to see if you had any news when I received your email. God is Awesome.

D.W. Amazing news!

B.D. To God be the glory!

M.E. Amen. Amen. Amen. And weeeee.

E.V. This email and praise report makes my heart scream with joy!!! God is so good, and his miracles are still so very present.

R.B. It is wonderful about the two-year-old. God loves little ones so much. They are His gift. I see something wonderful for this child.

D.B., HE does MIGHTY WORKS!!!
   That child has ALREADY done something special!!!
   Thank you! Thank you! Thank you for sharing this in such a timely way!!!

J.Z., I know sometimes terrible things happen to good people, but I do believe in the power of prayer. This is just another example! God blessed this young boy and God is GREAT!!! God Speed to all. Thank you for all you do, and God Speed Ministry.

Provision By Obedience:
The Ripple Effect

Tommy D'Aprile

IT ALL BEGAN with someone hearing God's urging. He heard it twice. He obeyed. That act of obedience began a miracle. A miracle not for him but for someone he may never meet.

Saturday, October 22, 2016: At the PDRA World Finals at Virginia Motorsports Park, Chaplain Tommy D'Aprile caught Chaplain Renee Bingham as she was walking up the steps toward the control tower.

"Here. God has prompted me twice to give you this hundred-dollar bill. You will know the need when you see it. I cannot wait to hear the story," he said with his big smile.

Renee placed the money in her wallet as a reminder each time she opened it to be watchful. She prayed for God to show her who the money was for. She expected it to be that weekend, but nothing. A week went by, and Renee still had the hundred-dollar bill. "Did I miss it, Lord?" she asked.

Saturday, November 5, 2016: As Renee was brushing her teeth, she sensed God. "You'll see her today." Renee was keenly alert for what lay ahead that day.

Gary and Renee Bingham were heading to Darlington Dragway in South Carolina for the "Junior Dragsters Racing 4 A Cause" charity event organized by Melissa Rabon. The event was rescheduled twice due to the weather. The new date allowed Gary and Renee to attend for the first time.

During the pre-race ceremony Melissa introduced the different children who were sponsored by the "Junior Dragsters Racing 4 A Cause." The stories were heart breaking. After Melissa shared each child's story and journey, Renee asked all the junior dragster kids to gather around them. She led them in prayer for these children which they repeated after her. It was a powerful and touching moment for everyone.

Later while walking through the pits, Gary and Renee saw Tracy pushing Shayna in her wheelchair. Shayna was one of the sponsored kids. "That's her," Renee heard God's whisper in her heart. "Tell her this hundred-dollar bill is a sign of my provision."

Renee introduced herself to Tracy and Shayna. Shayna was a normal two-year-old until a sinus infection led to serious disease. Shayna was in a coma for one-hundred-eight days. When she awoke, she could no longer talk and had limited motor skills. She could walk only short distances before tiring. Now, at age fifteen, her life was filled with doctors and her nights often with seizures.

Renee told Tracy how God had prompted Tommy to give this hundred-dollar bill and that it was a sign of God's provision for them. Tracy was stunned and thrilled.

Tracy & Shayna Evans with the $100

Renee thought it was done. Little did she know the miracle was only beginning.

Tracy and Shayna stopped by the God Speed Ministry display later to say thanks again. As they talked, Renee sensed a large black cloud over Tracy. She asked if she could pray for her. Tracy agreed. As Renee prayed and led Tracy in prayer the cloud disappeared. There was an audible sigh from Tracy as she clasped her hands to her heart. "The weight is gone!" she exclaimed joyfully. Her entire countenance and stance were different. Yea God!

Later Tracy stopped by again. Seeing God's work in her life, she began to share more of her story.

Shayna's dad left them on day four of the hospitalization.

Recently they had left the only man Shayna had known as dad when he began drinking. She moved into the home left to her and her two sisters by their mother, who died just this spring. The two sisters were already living there.

Shayna was bitten by one of the sister's dogs. She was hospitalized for injuries to her neck, ear, and head. She required seventy-two stitches.

The Department of Social Service would not allow Tracey and Shayna to go back into the home while the dog was still there. The sister chose the dog over her niece.

Tracy and Shayna were now homeless. They stayed in a hotel which used up her money and savings.

Tracy got sick and required surgery. When she got out of the hospital she stayed with a friend. She and Shayna slept on the floor.

Her vehicle was repossessed. Shayna was missing doctor's appointments.

Life was spiraling ever downward. She had no home, no car, and no hope when they left the "Junior Dragsters Racing 4 A Cause" event that day.

Sunday, November 6, 2016: Renee began to seek help from those locally. She asked for prayer on the God Speed Ministry Prayer email. God began to move. Someone paid for Tracy and Shayna to stay in the hotel for three nights. Calls, emails, and money began to come into God Speed for and Shayna.

Wednesday, November 9, 2016: A man in Oklahoma paid for a week in a hotel.

People in Missouri, Ohio and North Carolina sent money for a vehicle. A couple in North Carolina got their church involved.

Saturday, November 12, 2016: God Speed used the money donated to pay the down payment, insurance, tax, and tag for a 2009 Ford SUV for Tracey and Shayna.

Saturday evening: Tracey & Shayna have a vehicle and shelter but no food and no money. God Speed reached a local organization who delivered a box of food to them with enough for several days.

Monday, November 14, 2016: Tracey secured a home for her and Shayna.

Tuesday, November 15, 2016: The Evans duo moved into their new place.

Shayna now had home where she could get down on the floor and play, rest in her own bed and start this new chapter of life.

God did all of this in eleven days because of one man's obedience. His obedience began a ripple of provision centered around Tracey and Shayna in South Carolina but reached people in Florida, Oklahoma, Missouri, Ohio, North Carolina and South Carolina. Oh, the blessing of obedience!

Right Place, Gods Time

Chris Brackstone June 18, 2010

This is a topic that has people puzzled. I have seen things that look like they came together effortlessly without any help of man, (miracles) and then I see things that are the right place at the right time (divine appointments). Our human nature or flesh tends to say they are lucky or coincidences, but I tend to lean toward God's time.

> Psalm 139:16 *"All the days ordained for me were written in your book before one of them came to be."*

We can say that David, being the author, was speaking about himself. If David's days were known to God, are not our days as well? You do not have to be a pastor to minister to people, just have the faith and courage to go forward. When we think on the various times and places we have been, I think we could all agree there have been times God's hand was guiding us through a divine appointment.

One such appointment I recall was just last fall. I used to work as an electrician in the maintenance department for Ford three years ago. A foreman in my department on an opposite shift was nice and friendly. He was only forty years old then. I took the buy-out package in April 2007 and did not see him after that until one day in October of 2009. I got a call from a friend telling me this foreman had cancer. I thought about him and prayed for a door to open to meet with this guy and share Christ. I got his phone number and made the call. He was happy to hear from me and we set a time to meet for coffee.

When I went to see him, his mother and friends were there helping him. He was really medicated and not too mobile. He wanted to talk to me alone, so he asked me to drive him to the pizza shop to get lunch for his family. This would be my window to talk about God if he were open to hear.

As we got to the pizza place, they said it would be about twenty minutes before the pizza was ready. We stood outside and talked about his condition of cancer. The odds were not in his favor to beat it.

Then he shared about his life early in his youth. He told me about his grandfather being an enormous influence on him (he was a Pentecostal spirit filled believer). Then how, after college, he travelled to Asia where his Christian faith got confusing as he talked to people about their beliefs. He saw small villages worship false Gods.

The time was now for me to share the God I serve and tell him the truth about Jesus. I waited for directions from the Holy Spirit to speak the message he needed. As I shared, he said that he would feel like a hypocrite if he came back to Jesus. He felt others would not believe he was sincere because of his condition.

I prayed for a scripture to give him, and this is what the Lord shared with him; Mathew 20:1-16. It is the parable of the workers in the vineyard. Each worker started at various times in the day, but all received the same pay. This is like salvation. We all accept Christ at various times in our life but all who come to Jesus will receive the same pay (salvation). It does not matter what we have done or what we have, Jesus takes us just as we are.

Just two weeks later my friend passed away. I believe he met with God that day and know he is in Heaven. This is how I experience God moving through me. Others may find diverse ways, but you can see God working if you are open to him and follow the Holy Spirit in you. I would encourage you to take the time to know how Jesus is using you to minister to others. I run the race of life the best I can and when I fall short, Jesus carries me through.

Tasha's Testimony -June 2020

GOD HEALED ME from depression, anxiety disorders, major fear, disordered eating, and severe eczema and allergies which had been a fact of my life for ten years. For the past year, I have walked without these things and have instead experienced the immense joy of accepting my identity as a daughter of an extremely loving and gentle heavenly father.

Here is how it happened:

The "great struggle" began when I was eleven years old. Depression, fear, and anxiety crept into my life, bringing disordered eating along as well. I began to isolate myself as interacting with other people required a tremendous effort to reach into my energy reserves. It left me completely exhausted, so I preferred to be alone. I saw a counselor for a while and was prescribed with antidepressants (which I did not end up taking). Major academic perfectionism and anxiety attacks began in high school.

Physically, I had terrible eczema and allergies that prevented me from having any sort of sustainable fun. From the ages of sixteen to twenty-three, I had eczema constantly. It was always on my hands, and sometimes the nasty pustules would spread to my arms, my back, and my thighs. It was painful and my cracked skin would bleed onto my bed sheets. I could not touch anything acidic (oranges, tomatoes, etc.), and most soaps were off limits. I had awful allergies that made being outside for prolonged periods completely miserable. I could not be around dogs for very long because the allergic reaction would make it difficult for me to breathe.

I grew up with depression and anxiety. They became comfortable, and I had accepted them as extensions of my personality and identity. "I just have a personality that has a depressive tendency. I am just an anxious, nervous person. I am just a worrier. I am just a perfectionist. I cannot take failure."

Because I had grown up with them, I was used to them. The idea that I could exist without them was incomprehensible. It was scary. Without depression, without anxiety and fears, who would I be? I had mostly resigned myself to learning how to manage the depression and anxiety. I cultivated ways to cope with these things that I thought were just part of myself.

I had to get to the point of hating my situation so much that I wanted to do something about it. I had to get to the point where I no longer wanted to merely manage these things. The possibility that I did not have to live with this had to become real to me.

> 3 John 1:2–*Beloved, I wish above all things that thou mayest prosper and be in health, even as they soul prospereth.*

> 1 Thessalonians 5:23–*And the very God of peace sanctify you wholly; and I pray God your whole spirit and soul and body be preserved blameless unto the coming of our Lord Jesus Christ.*

The first thing that had to happen was that I had to believe that God wanted me to be healed now, in this life. None of this, "I will get my healing in heaven," because in heaven I will not have this body that I have now. I also had to accept that depression and anxiety did not fit into having a spirit and soul preserved blameless in the way 1 Thessalonians 5:23 says it should be. Maybe I was not supposed to have these things in my life after all!

I have had people administer the laying on of hands and pray for me sincerely in Jesus' name for physical healing. Nothing happened. This went on for a couple of years. Nothing ever happened. I have sought medical help for years to get rid of eczema and allergies. Nothing helped. Nothing even helped me manage it.

Psalm 138:2–*I will worship toward thy holy temple and praise thy name for thy lovingkindness and for thy truth: for thou has magnified thy word above all thy name.*

Psalm 138:2 says that God magnifies the Word above His own name. So many people had prayed for me in Jesus' name, but **I was not** necessarily going to the Word and seeking the truth as to what was causing the eczema. My priority was not seeking the truth in the Word and walking in obedience according to what is written in it. My priority was getting that healing. That is one of the reasons why healing prayers and laying on of hands were ineffective.

2 Timothy 1:7–*For God hath not given us the spirit of fear; but of power, and of love, and of a sound mind.*

1 John 4:18–*There is no fear in love; but perfect love casts out fear: because fear has torment. He that feareth is not made perfect in love.*

This fear (stress, anxiety, worry, phobias) was not from God. He did not give it to me. This depression was not from God. He did not give it to me. Because I am created in His image, this depression and fear were not part of my identity nor extensions of my personality. They were things that I had come into agreement with from an early age that latched onto me and robbed me of my true identity as a daughter of God.

Because perfect love casts out fear, having that fear meant that in an area of my life, I was not accepting God's love for me. I had believed lies that violated my identity. Instead of taking every thought captive to the obedience of Christ, I had entertained thoughts of self-deprecation, self-condemnation, rejection, pride, anxiety, and fear. I had entertained them, mulled over them, come into agreement with them, walked in obedience to them, and allowed them to become ingrained into my very being. They had wreaked havoc on my spirit, my soul, and my body for ten years.

First, I had to believe that God is a good Father, who loves me beyond measure, and who absolutely adores me because my heart is to be part of His kingdom. I had to separate myself from the depression and fear in my life. Although I had these things and had come to agreement with them, I had to assert that they did not define me. I had to revoke the ownership I had of it and stop calling it, "My depression, My eczema, etc."

I had to recognize the areas in my life in which I had the depression and anxiety and was not trusting God as my source. I had to acknowledge my role in participating with the depression and the anxiety. I had to repent to God for believing these lies about myself. I have no right to self-condemn or reject myself because I am a created being. I have no right to reject what God has created. To do that is to proclaim that God did not do a good job when He made me. I had to accept God's forgiveness. I also had to forgive myself. To be in un-forgiveness is to say that our standards are higher than God's.

Next, I had to renounce the depression and fear. I had to willfully fall out of agreement with them. Because I was seeking to walk in obedience according to God's Word, I could remove the spirits of depression and fear in Jesus' name. Because temptation does not go away, I had to resist the enemy when it has tried to come back by staying in the Word and making a conscious choice to walk in obedience according to what it says. I had to take thoughts captive and reject anything that is not in agreement with the truth.

Eczema and allergies are caused and exacerbated by fear, stress, and anxiety. When the depression and fear were removed, and my eyes were focused on my loving Father, the eczema and allergies were gone within a week. It has been over a year, and they have not come back. I can now use any soap

I want, slice tomatoes, eat oranges, and go backpacking out in various environments without any eczema or allergies. I now love being around people! There is no exhaustion in it at all, and I have no fear or anxiety about meeting new people. It is so much easier to try new things because extreme perfectionism is no longer there to keep me in fear of failure.

God is a loving Father who wants us to have fun. It is so much fun walking in obedience to His Word, which is not as complicated or as hard as the enemy would like us to think! The extreme fear I had blocked God's hand in my life and kept me from joy. It kept me from having so much fun. This past year has been the best I have had in my life! God has taken me to Alaska, the Pacific Northwest, the deserts of southern Utah, and to Iceland. I have discovered backpacking for the first time (something I can do now!) and have found so much joy in it! In Iceland, I worked at a dog sledding company and lived with fifty-nine dogs. It was one of the most meaningful experiences of my life, and I did not have any allergic reactions whatsoever!

This year has helped me develop a perfect hatred of evil, because for ten years it kept me from things I now enjoy and have come to love.

Best of all, I am getting to know God as my loving Father. I am becoming increasingly secure in my identity as His daughter. I am enjoying the daily process of sanctification as I become increasingly like my Dad. I love myself. I love who He created me to be. I not only enjoy being around other people, but I enjoy my own company as well because I no longer believe the lies!

1 John 1:7–*But if we walk in the light as He is in the light, we have fellowship one with another and the blood of Jesus Christ his Son cleanseth us from all sin.*

Proverbs 24:16–*For a just man falleth seven times, and riseth up again: but the wicked shall fall into mischief.*

Because I am learning to accept God's perfect love for me in all areas of my life, that fear is being cast out of me. To walk in the light is to be transparent and honest. We cannot hide anything when we are walking in the light; that means we need to be so secure that we will not even try to hide when we make mistakes. As Proverbs says, we rise again when we fall; we can find joy in repentance to our loving Father who is overjoyed in our willingness to participate with Him in our sanctification.

As I continue to be a doer of the Word and seek His truth, I know that life will get better and better despite the trials and temptations that will come. I am so excited for what will happen next! The enemy has had enough rule over my life; I do not want to give it any more place to rob me of joy.

Romans 2:11–*For there is no respect of persons with God.*

God is no respecter of persons. He does not show favoritism. What He did for me, He can also do for you. He WANTS to do it for you! It does not depend on being prayed for by one particularly "anointed" believer. It does not depend on the laying on of hands. It is straightforward, easily accessible, and entirely between you and God. He wants us to be sanctified wholly in our spirit, soul, and body TODAY. He is waiting for us to participate with Him in our sanctification. Get to it, saints! There is so much fun to be had!

(All scripture is Kings James Bible)

Van Abernethy's Testimony: My Defining Moment

I WAS TITHING MY normal amount, maybe a few pennies more. As a result, I was not begging for bread, just as the Lord promised. Missions, however, was something I totally let slide. One Sunday night, my pastor delivered a message on missions giving. God was touching my heart, and I knew it. You, of course, have heard that still, small voice yourself, so I do not have to explain it.

God burdened my heart for this cause, and effectively told me to double my tithe. Gulp! I have never wanted to argue my point with God so much in my life. I wrestled with it as I sat there in church, but finally decided that if God wanted me to do this (and I am certain He was dealing with me about it) then I figured He would supply, and I would just have to trust Him. I told God if he would supply, I would not fail to give the double portion beginning next Sunday.

Care to take a guess what happened next? Within a matter of days, the transmission in my truck came out. Did not see that one coming, did you? Ha! I am talking about a matter of a few days...before the following Sunday, and thus, before I even had the opportunity to do the "double portion thing" for the first time! Here is the crazy part: You might even argue the point that it was God (instead of the devil) who may have tinkered with my transmission. One thing is for sure, I will never believe that it was merely a coincidence.

I actually lean toward the crazy idea that maybe God was giving me a good reason to bail–just to test my faith–which was in fact beginning to falter at this point. Sometimes we give the devil too much credit in some areas, and clearly not enough in others. At any rate, I fixed the truck and went ahead and doubled my tithe the following Sunday, bringing my check book balance down to matter of a few dollars. Suddenly it seemed like I barely had two nickels to rub together...and I am supposed to double my tithes from now on? I barely had enough to do it once!

Suddenly, and I do mean suddenly, doors of opportunity in business begin to open...as if the floors of Heaven sprang a leak! God was showering my faith as I had never seen before...mainly because I had never stepped out on faith like this before. It is an amazing thing, but God has not stopped, so neither have I. I have continued to give the double portion every week since last summer, and God continues to provide to the point that it still takes me by surprise. His economy is gauged by a different barometer than say, the Gross Domestic Product, the unemployment rate or free trade.

Obviously, my faith has increased as a result. God has visited with me twice more (regarding tithe and offerings) since that initial Sunday night in church. I responded to His urging–this time without trying to rationalize the feasibility in my head. When you have seen the effects of faith up close, it is a lot easier to "step out" on faith again. God continues to bless; accordingly, consistently, and lovingly.

Van

GRAYSON MURPHY:
A SECOND CHANCE AT LIFE

By Grayson Murphy

MY ISSUES WITH heart problems started back in 2002. I had to have bypass surgery. The doctors said I needed a three-way bypass. When they went inside my chest, they ended up doing a five-way bypass. I prayed along with my family and friends that everything would go as planned and it did.

My bypass lasted until 2012 when I started having issues. I went to my cardiologist to get checked out. We started a new diet and medication regimens to try to contain the issues I was having. My heart started to deteriorate around 2014. I became worried because things were not working.

I decided to get a second opinion from another cardiologist. The day I went to see him, he said "We need to get you in the hospital to get some fluid off of you." I said, "Okay, when do we schedule to go?" "Right now!" So off I went.

They did a right-side catheterization on my heart. I had congestive heart failure with only five percent of my heart function on the left side. The doctor said I would be a viable candidate for LVAD (Left Ventricle Assist Device or heart pump.) I asked what would happen if I did not do that. The doctor said, "You would have about two weeks to live." "Well, that's a no brainer," I responded.

So, they put one in and kept me alive so I could go on the heart transplant list. That was in 2015 and on July 16, 2016, they called my wife's phone at 3:00 a.m. The number came up "caller unknown" so I told her not to answer it. Within three minutes, my phone rang with the same "Caller Unknown." I said, "I better answer it," and I am glad I did. It was the hospital calling, "We have an organ available for you if you want it."

"I'm on my way." Off we went to the INOVA Fairfax Hospital in Northern Virginia to get a new heart to replace my old worn out one.

When they took me in to prepare me for surgery, my family, and friends, and me, were praying for a successful operation. I woke up in the ICU in terrible pain due to the procedure. I was having a tough time dealing with the pain, so I prayed, asking God to make the pain go away. The pain started to subside until it was gone.

I was lying in my bed sleeping in my room the next day and I could feel someone holding my hand. When I opened my eyes, there was no one beside my bed and my hand was released. I guess my guardian angel was watching over me.

I never realized the power of prayer until I got home and found out all the family, friends, church friends and countless others who were praying for me. Prayer created the power for me to have a successful recovery and a new heart to keep me on the journey of life the Lord has put before me. I want to say thank you for all the prayers and well wishes I have received and continue to receive.

I am so sorry for the person who lost their life so I could have a second chance. I want to thank the donor family in their time of grieving for the loss of their loved one. I would encourage everyone to be an organ donor so someone else may have a second chance at life just as I did.

Again, thanks to God for giving me a good life, family, and friends.– Grayson Murphy

ANOINTED BY GOD FOR HEALING AND FULLNESS

GOD SPEED MINISTRY hosted two weeks of Abundant Life Day Camp for children near our headquarters in Kings Mountain, North Carolina. We partnered with therapists, healers, and a local church. Outdoor activities—hiking, fishing, and horseback riding- were held on the land of vision. The vision is for a facility where healing, restoration, and resurrection from the dead things in lives can occur.

The children experienced a miracle during the blessing on the hilltop where we worship. Renee Bingham held various anointing oils in her hands behind her back. As she held the oils, she could sense the oil God chose for each child. Once she knew which oil, she explained the purpose of that oil. She then spoke the blessing God gave for that child. One of the campers had been sexually abused by her father in years past. She was angry at her mother because her mother did not protect her. The oil drawn for her was myrrh.

"God has chosen the oil of myrrh for you," Renee spoke over her as she held the unopened bottle before the group of campers. "Myrrh is preparation to bury the old things of your life so that you may be raised into a new life. Today God offers to you a new way of living, a new lease on life."

Then Renee tried to open the bottle of oil. It was a bottle which she had used in the past, but the cap was stuck. She tried several times, but the cap was stuck tight. She handed the oil to the largest guy in the group. Everyone watched as he tried to open the bottle. The kids started to giggle. Then the girl said, "I can open it."

Renee sensed immediately that she would be able to open it. Renee took the oil and held it before the girl once again. "Yes, you will be able to open this bottle. God is showing you that only you can open your heart to let go of the past. Only you can open your heart to receive what he has for you." She handed the bottle of myrrh to the child who opened it easily with two fingers while the group marveled in awe.

Renee took the bottle of oil and cap. The stopper which allows the expensive oil to come drop by drop was out of the bottle and in the cap. Those stoppers require pliers to remove yet here it was in the cap. A greater stir went through the group as they saw the unstopped bottle. All sensed God's presence.

"God says you are to be as open as this bottle, to remove everything that blocks you from allowing His Holy Spirit to flow through you. Because He has removed this stopper as evidence of His desire to anoint you completely, I will pour this oil over your head rather than anointing you by finger on your forehead."

Renee Bingham anointing Abundant Life Camper

How the power of God fell upon that group of kids! How sweet and precious that time was in His presence. Those children encountered God in that experience. They KNEW He was with them that day. They have evidence of His pleasure, love, and compassion. God also gave them a cross in the clouds in the sky above. They KNOW Him in a new way.

Seven campers made professions of faith. Yea God!!!

BRIAN LAIR'S STORY

Excerpt from Brian Lair's blog.

BRIAN LAIR IS son of top sportsman racer Greg Lair of Texas. Brian was recently diagnosed with a malignant brain tumor and has undergone multiple brain surgeries to combat this disease. Despite his enduring trials, his attitude and his faith remain positive. Read an excerpt from his blog below and be encouraged.

Entry from August 20, 2008, www.brainlair.blogspot.com

Well.... I guess I should start off by saying sorry for taking so long to update this page. The past couple of days have been a whirlwind of activity. Anything is a whirlwind of activity after spending two weeks in a hospital bed. I was finally released from the Hospital on Tuesday afternoon and went straight to an appointment with a neuro oncologist in Dallas. The appointment went as well as I guess I could hope for. There is currently no cure for my cancer, however there are ways to kill most of it. This doctor suggested a combination of chemo and radiation that will start in the next few weeks. In the interest of getting a second opinion I am currently making plans to go down to M.D. Anderson in Houston to see another neuro oncologist there. My mother and I flew home Tuesday night as I have not left my house since. I feel like an elderly person with the number of pills I am required to take right now. I had to go out and get one of those pill organizer things just to keep them all figured out. I still have quite a bit of swelling in my head, so the headaches are constant. Other than the headaches, just an overall weak feeling are my only complaints. I am still waiting for the first person to make a Frankenstein comment which I am sure is soon to come. I cannot thank all of you, my family, and friends, for the support you have given me over the past couple of weeks. There is no way that I could have made it this far without all of you.

I have learned two main things over the past couple of weeks.

1. **GOD IS GREAT!!!**

2. Never take your friends and family members for granted because they will be there for you on your weakest days.

The next six months are going to tough, but I have an overall peace knowing that I have GOD, friends, and family on my side. This is nothing that I cannot handle. I am a fighter, and this is a fight that I have no doubt I am going to win. Please continue to keep me in your prayers and send positive thoughts my way. Thanks again for all your kind words of support and prayers. I cannot explain how much you all have helped me through this tough time. I look forward to seeing you all soon.

Entry from August 18, 2008

Just try to tell him NO....

After two long weeks.... Brian is scheduled to get out of the hospital tomorrow! YEAH!! He is so anxious to be in his own bed and for all the poking and prodding from the nurses to be over! His last couple of days have been great!

On Saturday night he decided that he wanted to go to church on Sunday morning. After asking several nurses and being rejected, Brian decided he was going to go regardless. The chief resident and a few nurses suggested that he go down to the chapel on the bottom floor of the hospital for a short service. What they did not understand was that Brian was going to leave the hospital and go to Irving Baptist Church in Irving. When Brian decides he is going to do something there is no stopping him! Brian told the nurses that he was going to church, and if they wanted, they could just think he was out on a long walk.

Brian got ready for church, and as we walked past the nurse's station, he told them he would be back shortly and reminded them not to miss him too much. He was equipped with his Bible, an IV port, a couple of hospital bracelets and two black eyes! He was ready for church!

Marshi, Greg, and Melissa met us there and we decided to sit close to the back so that Brian could avoid the mass of people and the descending stairs. This is an exceptionally large church and so we were basically in the nosebleed section! Brian's long legs did not agree with the close confines of the church seating, but besides a few leg cramps he did great!

At the end of the service Melissa and I went to the altar to pray during the closing songs. We soon felt a hand on our shoulders.... I figured it was a friend of mine who also attends the church and wanted to come pray with us. I was shocked to look up and see Brian!!! He knelt and prayed beside us. It was absolutely amazing! The fact that he walked all the way to the front by himself was incredible! God is so good!

THE PROVISION OF GOD —
EVAN KNOLL & BOBBY BENNETT

EVEN BEFORE I ever knew that there would be a God Speed Ministry, God spoke to my heart, telling me that if I ever had a ministry, I was not to do any kind of fundraisers. I was to depend totally upon Him as my Source for everything. He is my Heavenly Father and my Provider. I was not to doubt that He would take care of my needs or provide for me in every area.

God so impressed that upon me that it is in the by-laws of God Speed Ministry. This is His ministry, totally. He leads. He guides. He provides. But with all knowledge comes testing.

God Speed Ministry has made the commitment to cover every IHRA event: nationals, Pro Ams, bracket finals, junior dragster nationals. We stepped out on faith.

I really did not worry about the national events because I work for IHRA in the control tower. That covers my expenses and takes the burden off the ministry. Then IHRA decided not to take me to work the Rocky Mountain Nationals in Edmonton, Alberta, Canada. The ministry still needed to cover the event, but the cost would be substantial. After discussion with the board of directors, it was determined that God Speed would send me. We would trust God for provision. This had not caught Him off-guard. He knew this was coming, so He also knew the way through.

That decision was made on Wednesday or Thursday. The ministry had about $3000.00 in funds. We knew this decision would require a major part of this.

Then...

On Monday morning, about 8:30 a.m., I received a phone call from Evan Knoll of Torco Racing Fuels and Bobby Bennett of Torco Competition Plus.

com. Evan stated that he knew the cost of fuel and wanted to do something to help God Speed. "I want to give the ministry $5000.00 to help with traveling expenses."

I sank to my knees in tears of gratitude and awe. Evan could have stated that he wanted to donate to the ministry and let it go at that. But he specifically stated, "... to help with travel expenses." Only God and the board of directors knew of our need to travel to Edmonton.

God laid it on Evan's heart and placed the words in His mouth to specifically minister to this ministry. God is faithful. God is good.

We please God by believing; believing that He is, believing that He rewards those who seek Him, believing His Word is true, believing and trusting Him to be our Heavenly Father.

> *"If you then, who are evil, know how to give good gifts to your children, how much more will the heavenly Father give the Holy Spirit to those who ask him!"* Matthew 7:11f[10]

I do not know where you are today, but I know where God is and what He can do. He is greater than anything we face. Trust Him.

---

[10] The ESV® Bible (The Holy Bible, English Standard Version®) is adapted from the Revised Standard Version of the Bible, copyright Division of Christian Education of the National Council of the Churches of Christ in the U.S.A. All rights reserved.

Billy Corker: Life Led by the Spirit

Steve Corker, dad Billy Corker, wife Brenda Corker

BILLY CORKER IS Steve Corker's father. Steve Corker is an IHRA Top Sportsman World Champion. Steve and his wife Brenda were the first Board of Directors members for God Speed Ministry. Steve and Brenda were also the national Worship Leaders for God Speed for twelve years. The following stories are from Billy, who lives his life led by Holy Spirit.

Back a year or so ago I was tilling in my garden when the screw came out of the pully. It ruined that pully. When I tried to replace the pully, it would not go on the shaft. I tried everything I could think of, but nothing worked. I even took a hammer and tried to bump it on, but it would not go.

I went to the mailbox on the way to the house to get a cup of coffee. In the mail was a letter from God Speed Ministry. Inside was a card with a prayer on it just for me. I read the prayer and drank my coffee.

When I returned to that tiller, I took that pulley and so help me God, that pulley slid right on that shaft with no resistance at all. God is good. Prayer works!

Billy Corker

I was thinking about Job and his friends in the Bible. I noticed Job got relief when he prayed for his friends.

A year or so ago my upper back began to hurt. I went to the doctor who sent me for x-rays. They showed two or three discs were bad which were causing the pain.

I had a friend at church who also had back pain. As I walked into church, the Holy Spirit reminded me of Job. I went up to my friend, under the prompting of the Holy Spirit, and said, "I will pray for your back and neck. God will heal both of us."

My friend had plans for surgery that never happened. It has been ten years since I have had no back or neck pain.

God is so good!

I went to work at 7:30 a.m. in my back yard. The grass was tall. I stopped for lunch and was watching TV about 1:40 p.m. when I noticed I was missing one of my hearing aids. I had worked in the back yard, the garden, as well as weed eaten around the electric fence where the grass was ten inches tall. I looked in the house. All to no avail. I had no clue where I lost it.

I called my friend of over forty years. His name is Holy Spirit. He is the best friend I have ever had. I said to Him, "I know you know where it is and can take me to it."

He said, "OK. Come on, let's go find it."

As we were walking through my yard, suddenly, He stopped. I reached down in the grass and picked up my hearing aid. I let out a yell of praise to God.

Holy Spirit knows everything. He works with people who know Him and will listen to His voice and obey it.

A Miracle at the Corker farm

I had a few cows on my farm. One of my cows had a large growth on her eye lid. My son, Steve, saw the growth and said, "Dad, get a vet to come remove that growth from that cow's eye lid."

I said, "No. I cannot give that cow to a vet. You know as well as I do that a vet will charge me more than the cow is worth!"

A day or two later I walked up to that cow and laid my hand on her head. I cursed that growth in Jesus' Name and demanded that growth to leave my cow's eye and do not ever come back.

Three days later I was walking by that cow and noticed the growth was gone. And it did not even leave a scar! God is so good. Amen!

Redeemed from the curse of pain.

I went to the hospital and had four bypasses. They also cleaned out the main vein in my neck. I was in the hospital for six days. When the doctor looked at my chart, there was no medicine for pain listed. If we are redeemed from something, then we do not have it.

Listen to the Holy Spirit (A North Carolina Miracle)

My job there was to keep all our workers supplied with material. With that in mind, I was driving down the road when a thought came to my mind, "Why don't you check the house off the next road?" I decided to obey my thoughts.

When I reached the house, I noticed the homeowner's wife standing outside her car. I pulled up and asked her if all was ok.

She said, "I left my keys in the car. When I closed the door all the doors locked!" Her small child was still in the car. The temperature was ninety-eight degrees.

I asked her if she called for help. "Yes," she said, "they should be here any minute."

I said, "I am going to check the house," and walked away.

When I entered the house, the Holy Spirit yelled at me, "Are you not going to get that child out of that car?!!!"

I said, "Oh yes Sir, yes Sir." I had my hammer in my hand. As I was going toward the car, I picked up a piece of metal stripping. I stopped by my truck and got a pair of snipers.

When I reached the car, I decided to put God first. "Door, you are a name and lock, you are a name, and the name of Jesus is above every name." Then I said aloud, "Door lock, I command you to unlock now in the name of Jesus."

As I turned to work on my jig, the lady said, "I heard a click." She reached and pulled the door open.

Now all you skeptics just as well go ahead and say AMEN. This lady stood up in her Baptist Church and testified, saying, "I am thirty years old, and I've seen my first real live miracle."

Now everybody listen close: "That child could have died if I had not heard the voice of God. I was there at the house for about an hour. No help ever showed up!"

A Transformed Life (North Carolina Miracle #Two)

There in North Carolina, we had a man who was one of the original groups called Hell's Angels working with us. One day I walked up beside him, laid my hand on his shoulder, and said, "Son, I want to tell you something." His name was Ron. "Ron, I want you to know that I love you and God loves you."

Big, and I do mean BIG, tears ran down his face. He looked at me and said, "Pop, nobody ever told me that.... nobody."

He lived next door to my son Steve. I asked him to bring his family over to my son's house that night. "We have a Bible Study every week there. If you come and do not like it, I will not ask you again."

They came that night and the whole family was born again. They started attending church. They still serve God.

Note: about three days after they were saved, my son stopped me and said, "I don't think Ron was saved because he is still smoking pot." I told him we had better let God take care of Ron. About two or three days later, Ron stopped me and said, "Pop, I was smoking a joint last night and a voice spoke aloud and said, 'You do know that you are blowing that smoke in My face, don't you?"

That ended the pot smoking. Praise God!

We were having a Bible Study at our house once a week. This couple came with their three kids. One day at noon, we were eating lunch when the phone rang. It was this lady saying her son had broken his leg. They lived only a short distance away, so we went over and prayed for the boy. We bound Satan and asked for a supernatural healing.

The lady said the doctor was going to put that leg in a cast after lunch. We had to get back to work, so we told the lady we would be back later that afternoon.

We went back about eight o'clock. When we arrived se saw the little boy had no cast on his leg. He was running up and down the staircase.

We do not know what really happened, but God knows. That is all we need to know.

———————————

Brian and his helper were always on time for work. But today they were late. A few minutes later, his helper called to say Brian was in the emergency room at the hospital. They thought it was kidney stones and they may not make it to work that day.

The hospital was thirty minutes away. Now here is what I told him. "Go back in there and tell him Pop said the stones are dissolving." His helper went back there and told him what I said that the stones were dissolving. The helper hung up the phone. Forty-five minutes later they arrived at the job, ready to work.

The church is crying for help. Watch this: If God's people keep their mouths shut, these miracles would not be happening. I do not know about you, but when I see a need, I cannot keep my mouth closed and just pretend I do not see the need. This is where the Holy Spirit comes in to help and gives you and me the gift needed to meet that need.

Note: The gifts only come when there is a need. I believe any Spirit filled Christian can operate in all nine of the gifts of the Spirit when needed.

HOW MY BROTHER DEFEATED COLON CANCER

My brother was diagnosed with colon cancer, and he accepted the doctor's words as a bad report. The doctor scheduled surgery at a medical center in Little Rock, AR. At that time, I lived in Crossett, Arkansas, over one-hundred-twenty-five miles away. My brother had no other family but me and one other brother.

On the day of surgery, I got up at three o'clock in the morning to get to Little Rock in time to pray for him before the surgery. I stood in his hospital room and cursed that cancer and commanded it to die at the roots and come out of him in Jesus' name.

Two nurses came into the room to take him to surgery, but first they had to mark his side where the bag would be in his reach. I told them he would not have that bag. But they said we must mark the spot anyway. I know the nurses thought I was rude, but they lived to see what I said happen. They took him off to surgery. Later his doctor came and told me they felt sure they got all the cancer and that he did not have the bag.

I would take him to Little Rock for his checkups. If you have ever been in that hospital, you know that the waiting room will seat about fifty people.

Six weeks later I took him for his checkup. When they called his name, they took him back to a small office. When he came back to the waiting room his face was white as a snowball. I said, "what in the world did they say?" (I want everyone to listen closely as to what happened next.)

He said they told him the cancer was back. I jumped up out of my chair and said, "you go back in there and tell them they are wrong because I cursed that cancer in Jesus' name, and it is dead."

I sat back down. Remember what I said back in his room on the day of surgery? I am about to show you a key about operating in the gifts of the Spirit.

All those people looked at me like I had just got out of an insane hospital. Now here is what I want you to see. I could care less what those people thought or said one to another. Jesus said you say to the mountain. He did not tell me to ask Him to speak to the mountain. I spoke to the mountain cancer, and it died at the roots.

Watch this. You cannot operate in the things of God as long as you consider what other people think or say. I told that cancer to die at the roots and come out of him.

Here is what happened. They ran every test in the book for at least a year or more on my brother. There was never even a trace of the cancer.

The Bible says all things are possible to them that believe. Do not back off what you say!

I wondered if my son was hearing anything I was saying. His name is Billy Jr. We worked together for years, and every day I would tell him how much God loved him and how Jesus gave us authority to call the angels to our aid if we need them. I explained to him that being filled with the Holy Spirit was the way we obtained that power. Now just to be completely honest, I was not sure he heard a word I said.

A year or so later he met this lady and her son who was living at a deer camp. Some of this lady's family were members of that deer club. She needed a place to stay so her family arranged for her and her son to stay there. Not long after she and her son moved into that camp, one night at about nine o'clock her son went into what she called a fit. He screamed out and she could not restrain or hold him. He was so frightened. That went on for hours and this happened every few days.

Then she met Billy Jr. at the grocery store and asked him to spend the night with them. The first night everything was calm. Billy was going to leave, and she began to beg and cry saying, please stay another night. He finally agreed.

The next night at about nine or ten o'clock the little boy began to fret and then began to scream and run. My son and the mother could not hold him. He was so frightened. Billy said he went to the window and looked out. He saw five or six people out there that looked like men, but they were demons.

Here is my surprise. My son called out to the angels for help. They came, seven or eight of them. When Billy looked out the window, he saw these angels running after the demons. In just a few minutes the boy was back to normal. Billy and the lady began to praise God and thank the angels. Billy later shared this story at our church.

PS: you never know which words will be heard.

KATHY FISHER'S STORY

By Kathy Fisher

OFTEN IN MY prayers, I ask that if the Lord wants us to continue to race that He will show us the way. What happened for us over the last month was way beyond what I could have ever expected. To this day I am still just blown away.

I met Pete Hunt a little over a year ago through my work with Frank Hawley's Drag Racing School. Pete, who hails from Sarnia, Ontario, Canada, acquired his competition license last summer during a class at Norwalk.

Pete and I have stayed in touch since through emails and a few phone calls. I do not think we had spoken for a couple of months.

It was just a few short weeks ago that Pete was surfing the internet when he came across my Top Alcohol licensing videos on YouTube. He decided to look at our website.

Through our conversations, Pete knows how much I absolutely love to race in Canada. When Pete saw that we did not have the Grand Bend event on our schedule again this year, he knew I must be disappointed. But it was seeing the God Speed Ministry logo on our website, he felt moved to do something to help us.

Pete sent us a card. "Kevin and Kathy, come on north and burn some of our 'horsepower producing' Canadian air. Here are some 'Bend Bucks' for the nationals. Hope to see you, Pete."

I was absolutely speechless! Ask anyone – that is an accomplishment for anyone to make that happen.

Although I was scheduled to work that weekend, everything worked out so my husband Kevin and I could go to Grand Bend. What happened from there was nothing but continued blessings.

Not only did we all have an absolute blast throughout the entire weekend, but it was so cool to go to the finals and have Pete join us in the winner's circle pictures. (And now enough winnings to make it to our next race!! WOW! Praise God!) Add to the excitement, one of my bosses, Frank Hawley, attended the Grand Bend event. This was the first time Frank had ever seen me race.

All of this was not just 'good luck.' It was not something just 'really cool' that happened. This was all God's plan. I just smile every time I think of how truly good He is to us!

PRAISE GOD for all He gives us every day! Not just in situations like this, when His blessings are so obvious, but **EVERY SINGLE DAY in ALL that HE provides for us!**

Thanks to Pete's kindness, we had more than enough to cover our expenses for the event. The remainder of the funds was passed on to God Speed Ministry, where they can continue to provide others as they have provided for us!

What an abundance of blessings all wrapped up into one!

Don Garlits-
In his Own Words

Chaplain Rich Guy had a conversation with Don Garlits, a seventeen-time World Champion, back in 2020 about Don's faith. This is what he had to say.

> *"When I was six or seven years old, the family that lived next door to us, in 1938, were black, and the old black man's name was Robert Henry. And he said to me, and his son, who was my age, Robert Henry junior. We had been out in a field, probably doing something we weren't supposed to be doing, like hitting the corn with sticks, not real serious, bet we shouldn't have been doing it. I'll never forget his words, (Mr. Henry), he said "Boys, don't ever do anything that will make it hard on you when you get over to the other side." And I have lived my whole life by that. That is one of the greatest pieces of wisdom.*
>
> *I was baptized at fourteen, but I drifted away as I got older, but then I married my wife in 1952, and she was a very Christian person, and she helped me get back on track. God has always been a part of my life since then, and I couldn't get through life without Him."*

THE ACCIDENT

On March 8, 1970, at Lions Drag Strip, Garlits was driving his front-engine slingshot rail dragster, when the vehicle suffered a catastrophic failure. The two-speed transmission Garlits was developing exploded and took a piece out of his right foot as the car literally broke in half. Don related how he had to rely on God's mercy to get him through.

"When I was laying in the hospital with my foot blown off, I had a lot of pain. I didn't want to take the pain killer because I had a bad episode when I was severely burned in an accident in 1959, and it took me over a year to get off them. So, I was really having a tough time in the hospital in California with the pain. It was just unbelievable, the pain, and I didn't want to take those pain killers. So, I just cried out to God, "Please help me!" And miraculously, He did. A warmth came over me, and I felt loved. And I didn't have any more pain for the rest of my healing period. And you know, I have talked to several people who didn't want to take pain killers, and they cried to God for help, just like me, and He did help them. They had exactly the same experience."

After the 1970 season ended, Don Garlits designed and built a mid-engine dragster, which would be safer to drive. The car was an enormous success, winning several races, and it revolutionized the sport of Drag Racing.

To make God known among all motorsport's nations.

**To glorify God and Him only, celebrating
Him in every word, thought and action.**

My life is a roadway directing others to God through Christ. I will use my mouth to glorify God. I will speak His praises, His glory, His kingdom rule in heaven, on this earth and in my life. I repent of all the times when I have employed my mouth in other ways such as complaining, criticizing, or amplifying what the enemy is attempting to do in people or in this world. It is a mindset which I chose this day because......

I have the mind of Christ. My thoughts are His thoughts. I quickly evict any thought which sets itself against God's rule and reign. I look to God to see what He is doing in the situation and then I proclaim His work over it.

God Speed Ministry logo

God Speed Ministry Chaplains

Founder Gary Bingham   March 28, 2004–present
Founder Renee Bingham   March 28, 2004 – present

2004

Steve Corker	April 2004 – December 31, 2013
Brenda Corker	April 2004–December 31, 2013
Rev. Bill Dickerson	May 2004 – March 8, 2018
Christy Bingham Rice Greek	October 2004 – October 2007
Rev. Jerry Blazier	November 2004 -October 2023

2005

Joe Sannutti	February 2005–present
Debbie Sannutti	February 2005–present
Lisa Bingham Collier	February 2005- December 2018
Rev. Floyd West	February 2005 – December 2008
Diana West	February 2005 – December 2008
Rev. Scott	March 2005 – December 2007
Greer Scott	March 2005 – December 2007
Matt Zapp	April 2005 – present
Deborah Tankersley	June 2005 – December 31, 2019
Roger Hallead	July 2005 – December 31, 2010

2006

Stuart Smith	February 2006 – November 2016
Sylvia Maedgen	February 2006 – November 2016
Joey Keith	February 2006 – December 31, 2019

Diana Keith   February 2006 – December 31, 2019
Rev. Mike Imhoff   April 2006 – present
Michelle Michael   April 2006- December 31, 2015
Rev. Steve Longmire   June 2006–present

2007
Chic LaNasa   April 2007 – present
Carol Rix   April 2007- December 31. 2015
Matt Robinson   April 2007 – March 2016

2008
Anna Janette Guy   April 2008 – November 2022
Richard Guy   April 2008 – November 2022
Diane Ellis   August 2008 – December 31, 2010

2009
Pattie Head   April 2009 – December 31, 2019

2010
Jim Wilburn   November 2010–present

2011
Matt Collier   April 30, 2011- December 2018
Keith Petersen   August 2011- present

2014
Kenny Bomar   September 19, 2014–present
Tommy D'Aprile   March 24, 2014 – present
Neal Muylaert   September 2014- December 31, 2019

2015

Allen Furr	April 2, 2015 – March 4, 2024
Roger Rigg	September 29, 2015 – December 31, 2019
Rev. Sean Cooper	November 25, 2015 – December 31, 2019

2016

Rev. Glenn Head	February 2016 – December 31, 2019
Don Patterson	February 2016–September 2018
Jean Patterson	February 2016–September 2018

2022

Ashley Allen	February 6, 2022 – March 4, 2024
David Merrill	September 2022 – February 27, 2024
Tammie Smith	December 2022 – present

2023

| Rev. Greg Parker | August 2023 – present |

God Speed Ministry Chaplains and family 2009. Left to right: Front Row: Jean Dickerson, Sylvia Maedgen, Matt Zapp, Isaac Zapp, Haley Zapp, Luke Zapp, Jane Miller. 2nd Row: Pattie Head, Lisa Bingham (Collier), Renee Bingham, Janette Guy, Rebecca Smith, Carol Rix, Debbie Sannutti. Back Row: Gene Head, Gary Bingham, Bill Dickerson, Richard Guy, Stuart Smith, Tom Rix, Joe Sannutti, Joey Keith.

God Speed Chaplains 2012 inviting you to become a chaplain. Left side front row: Rebecca Smith, Debbie Sannutti, Brenda Corker, Renee Bingham. Left Side 2nd row: Stuart Smith, Joe Sannutti, Steve Corker, Gary Bingham. Back Jerry Blazier. Right side front row: Bill Dickerson, Christy Greek, Howard Michael, Chic LaNasa, Lisa Collier. Right 2nd Row: Mike Imhoff, Michelle Michael, Larry McLaughlin, Matt Collier.

God Speed Ministry 2017 Conference. Left to right: Anita & Harold Honeycutt, Gary Bingham, Mike Imhoff, Diana & David Merrill, Chic LaNasa, Pattie & Gene Head

Chaplain Tammie Smith ministers at the PDRA

Chaplain Greg Parker ministering at the Spring Fling at GALOT Motorsports Park

Chaplains Diana & Floyd West, first Division 5 Chaplains

Chaplain Kenny Bomar

Chaplain Tommy D'Aprile ministering to driver before he runs

Rainbow over the pits of an IHRA Darlington Event

MUSIC MINISTRY
THROUGH THE YEARS

Steve & Brenda Corker - National Worship Leaders

Steve & Brenda Corker leading worship

Kayla Archer

Ethan Atkinson

Kimmie Benton

Cindi Bowen

Broken Vessel

Clay Bullard

Reggie Burnett

Gordon & Brenda Cole

Anthony Davis & Peter – New Community Church

Jeannie Doss

Charles Edwards

Randy Ferrell – Cross Road
Ministries

Ronnie Forrester

Carol Gilbert

Rita Hall

Lexi Howell

Ivey Hutto

Barry McGee – BarryMcGee.com

MS Givens

Harmony

Glenn Head

Francine Johnson

Becky McFadden

Jacob McLamore

Michael Norris

Josh Pepper

Tara Phillips

Resolution Dance Group

Morgan & Lexi Rhinehart

Curt Rochan

Rock Solid Band

Tyler Sears

Sean Shultis

Kelly Smith

Linda Smith

Rebecca Smith

Son Rise Band

Tim Sowards

Debbie Stirret

Jerry & Amy Stoddard

Case Stott

Laurel Tankersley

Savannah Tankersley

Joel Thomas

Marie Waller

Shannon Waycaster

Samantha Wilson

Tedra Yawn

CONTRIBUTORS

Van Abernethy

Gary Bingham

Renee Bingham

Chris Brackstone

Lisa Collier – National InVision Youth Director

Matt Collier–National InVision Youth Director

Allen Cook – 1320 Web Services

Rusty Cook

Theresa Cook

Billy Corker

Tommy D'Aprile – Pro Racer, Division 2 Chaplain, PDRA Chaplain

Casey Davis

Bill Dickerson – Division 4 Chaplain, Director

Kathy Fisher

Don Garlits – Big Daddy

Christy Greek

Richard Guy – Division 1 Chaplain, Director

Gene Head

Glenn Head–Division 9 Chaplain

Pattie Head–Division 9 Children's Chaplain. National Kid's On Track Director

Bobby Hicks

Ted & Suzanne Hunt

Mike Imhoff–Division 3 Chaplain, Director

Brian Lair

Chic LaNasa–Division 3 Chaplain

Jack Larsen

Grayson Murphy

Keith Petersen – Division 6 Chaplain, Director

Joe Sannutti–Division 2 Chaplain

Greg & Gina Slack

Deborah Tankersley–Division 2 Children's Chaplain

Tasha

Marie Waller – Singer

Jim Wood – IHRA official / Racer

Mentions

Abilene Dragstrip

Bill Bader – IHRA Owner and President

Bobby Bennett – Competition Plus.com

Jerry Blazier – Division Four Chaplain

Kenny Bomar–Division Two Chaplain, Memphis Int'l Raceway
    track chaplain

Bradenton Motorsports Park

CCRA – Carolina Class Racers Association

Castrol Raceway

Cameron Choate

Jaime Choate

Lloyd Scooter Choate

Christian & Missionary Alliance Church

Sean Clevenger

Ailey Collier

Everleigh Collier

Billy Corker Jr.

Brenda Corker – National Music Leader

Steve Corker – National Music Leader

Donnie Crowder – IHRA Official

Thomas Czaplicki–IHRA official

Dallas Raceway Park

Jean Dickerson – Wife of Bill Dickerson

Dan Driscoll – IHRA Consultant

Ronnie Davis

Doug Herbert Performance Center

Jim Edlin

Tracy & Shayna Evans

Kevin Fisher

Frank Hawley's Drag Racing School

Ashley Franklin – daughter of Tommy & Judy Franklin

Judy Franklin – Owner of the PDRA

Tommy Franklin – Owner of the PDRA

Mike Fulfer – Division Four Chaplain for Racer's For Christ (RFC)

Scott Gardner – IHRA President

Grand Bend Motorplex

Elliott Gragg – Son of Satch Gragg

Satch Gragg – IHRA Starter, IHRA Race Director

Tony Gray

Landon Greek

Eugene Grigg – Attorney

Janette Guy – Division One Children's Chaplain

Bob Harris – PDRA President

Scott Heaton – IHRA announcer

Doug Herbert – Top Fuel Racer, owner of Doug Herbert
    Performance Center

Michael Hunt

Pete Hunt

Ren Hunt

Houston Raceway Park

Immokalee Regional Raceway

IHRA – International Hot Rod Association

Wesley Jones

Joey Keith – Division Four Chaplain, Christian Outreach Racers
    Evangelism- C.O.R.E.

Sam Kearns

Kinston Dragstrip

Marc Kinton – IHRA Safety Director

Robert Kinton – IHRA Official

Evan Knoll – TORCO Race Fuels

Frank Kohutek – IHRA Division Four, Six, Seven Director

Greg Lair

Larry Langley

Jimmy Lewis

Junior Dragsters Racing 4 A Cause

Steve Longmire – Division Four Chaplain

Lonestar Raceway

Loose Rocker Promotions

Lufkin Raceway

Sylvia Maedgen – Division Four Children's Chaplain

Tommy Maedgen – helper/racer Division Four

Travis Mangum – Public Accountant

Roger Marsh–National Fellowship of Raceway Ministries

Maryland International Raceway

Larry McLaughlin

Michelle McLaughlin

Montgomery Motorsports Park

Mountain Park Dragstrip

MRO – Motor Racing Outreach

Neal Muylaert–Division Seven Chaplain, Director

NFRM–National Fellowship of Raceway Ministries

NHRA–National Hot Rod Association

Norwalk Raceway Park- now Summit Motorsport Park

Pat O'Connor – Jim Edlin's friend

Roland Osborne – Founder Christian Motorsports Illustrated Magazine

Skooter Peaco–IHRA

Aaron Polburn – IHRA Vice-President

Thomas Pope – Journalist

PDRA – Professional Drag Racers Association

Melissa Rabon

RFC – Racers For Christ

Christy Bingham Rice (Greek)– National Children's Chaplain

Levi Rice

Carol Rix – Division Five Chaplain, Director

Tom Rix – Super Stock Racer

Matthew Robinson–Division Nine InVision Chaplain

Rockingham Dragway

San Antonio Raceway

Debbie Sannutti – Division Twp Children's Chaplain

Alan Savage

SWJDA – SouthWest Junior Dragster Association

Staging Light Events

Susan Smith

Tammie Smith – PDRA & Division Two Chaplain

Summit Motorsport Park

Joe Tankersley

Laurel Tankersley

Texas Motorplex

Bruce Thrift

Scott Trent – RFC Chaplain

Ian Tocher–Journalist

Tulsa Raceway Park

US 131 Motorsports Park

Virginia Motorsports Park

Wanda Weikel

Diana West – Division Five Chaplain

Floyd West – Division Five Chaplain, Director

Jim Wilburn – Division Four Chaplain

Connie Wood

WDRA – World Drag Racing Alliance

Matt Zapp – Division Three Chaplain, Director; & Division One Chaplain, Director; Division Nine Chaplain